# Common Sense

# Common Sense

✦

or

## Why
## Not to Look at the World
## throughColored Glasses,
## Two Toilet Paper Rolls,
## and Some Scotch Tape

*J. P. Hingst*

iUniverse, Inc.

New York  Lincoln  Shanghai

## Common Sense
### or Why Not to Look at the World throughColored Glasses, Two Toilet Paper Rolls, and Some Scotch Tape

iUniverse books may be ordered through booksellers or by contacting:

iUniverse
2021 Pine Lake Road, Suite 100
Lincoln, NE 68512
www.iuniverse.com
1-800-Authors (1-800-288-4677)

Because of the dynamic nature of the Internet, any Web addresses or links contained in this book may have changed since publication and may no longer be valid.

The views expressed in this work are solely those of the author and do not necessarily reflect the views of the publisher, and the publisher hereby disclaims any responsibility for them.

ISBN: 978-0-595-46578-1 (pbk)
ISBN: 978-0-595-90874-5 (ebk)

Printed in the United States of America

# Contents

Acknowledgments . . . . . . . . . . . . . . . . . . . . . . . . . . . . . . . . . . . . . . . vii

Where Am I Coming From? . . . . . . . . . . . . . . . . . . . . . . . . . . . . . 1

What Team Do You Play For? . . . . . . . . . . . . . . . . . . . . . . . . . . 4

Our Founding Fathers . . . . . . . . . . . . . . . . . . . . . . . . . . . . . . . . 8

Politics and Politicians . . . . . . . . . . . . . . . . . . . . . . . . . . . . . . . 14

Political Crimes . . . . . . . . . . . . . . . . . . . . . . . . . . . . . . . . . . . . . . 16

Politicians and Focus . . . . . . . . . . . . . . . . . . . . . . . . . . . . . . . . . 28

Political Taxes and Fines . . . . . . . . . . . . . . . . . . . . . . . . . . . . . . 33

Spinning the Numbers . . . . . . . . . . . . . . . . . . . . . . . . . . . . . . . . 36

The Media . . . . . . . . . . . . . . . . . . . . . . . . . . . . . . . . . . . . . . . . . . . 43

The Attack on Tobacco . . . . . . . . . . . . . . . . . . . . . . . . . . . . . . . . 51

Lawyers and Law . . . . . . . . . . . . . . . . . . . . . . . . . . . . . . . . . . . . . 62

Insurance Companies . . . . . . . . . . . . . . . . . . . . . . . . . . . . . . . . . 65

For the Greater Good . . . . . . . . . . . . . . . . . . . . . . . . . . . . . . . . . 69

Socialism . . . . . . . . . . . . . . . . . . . . . . . . . . . . . . . . . . . . . . . . . . . . 72

Performing Arts and Socialism . . . . . . . . . . . . . . . . . . . . . . . . . 75

Religion and Socialism . . . . . . . . . . . . . . . . . . . . . . . . . . . . . . . . 77

Police and Privilege . . . . . . . . . . . . . . . . . . . . . . . . . . . . . . . . . . 82

Educate or Legislate . . . . . . . . . . . . . . . . . . . . . . . . . . . . . . . . . . 84

Homeowners' Associations. . . . . . . . . . . . . . . . . . . . . . . . . . . . . . . . . . . 90

Discrimination. . . . . . . . . . . . . . . . . . . . . . . . . . . . . . . . . . . . . . . . . . . . 95

Why Do Descendants of Slaves Vote for Slavery? . . . . . . . . . . . . . . . . 98

Overall Attack on the Poor . . . . . . . . . . . . . . . . . . . . . . . . . . . . . . . . . 101

Global Warming . . . . . . . . . . . . . . . . . . . . . . . . . . . . . . . . . . . . . . . . . 106

Gun Control . . . . . . . . . . . . . . . . . . . . . . . . . . . . . . . . . . . . . . . . . . . . 116

Patriot Act. . . . . . . . . . . . . . . . . . . . . . . . . . . . . . . . . . . . . . . . . . . . . . 121

Recent News and Reactions. . . . . . . . . . . . . . . . . . . . . . . . . . . . . . . . 124

Bullying. . . . . . . . . . . . . . . . . . . . . . . . . . . . . . . . . . . . . . . . . . . . . . . . 134

Business and Industry . . . . . . . . . . . . . . . . . . . . . . . . . . . . . . . . . . . . 142

Government Medical Insurance. . . . . . . . . . . . . . . . . . . . . . . . . . . . . . 154

Miscellaneous Ideas . . . . . . . . . . . . . . . . . . . . . . . . . . . . . . . . . . . . . . 160

Conclusion . . . . . . . . . . . . . . . . . . . . . . . . . . . . . . . . . . . . . . . . . . . . . 169

# *Acknowledgments*

I would like to take this opportunity to thank Heather Burke, the daughter of a friend, for starting me thinking about this book by asking me if I thought that life was more difficult now than when I was growing up. Heather also read early drafts of the book and gave encouragement to continue the project. Thank you. Also thanks to William Velasco, a student who lives next door, for talking to me for well over an hour about the political situation of the country and the direction it is heading. William also read an early draft and gave encouragement to the book. The discussions with these two people convinced me that the younger generation does not have a frame of reference for our current political situation. William was quite surprised at the things we discussed and thought that I had some good insight into many problems.

There are others who I need to thank for giving me input and ideas. I would like to thank Phil Marchant for the story about his sister and her traffic ticket. I would also like to thank Jim ValDez for his giving me several stories.

I would also like to thank my girlfriend, Betty-Jo Blank, for putting up with my requests to read and comment on the various topics in the book. Also, thanks to her friend Sharlee Burke for being supportive of the book. All of these people read early drafts and felt I was making some good and important points, and they all gave encouragement to continue.

Thank you all.

# Where Am I Coming From?

Over the past few months, I have been asked by some younger people about my thoughts on the changes in our country over the years and where I think it is heading. This could be because they feel my sixty-plus years give me some knowledge about the changes I've seen. They have engaged me in several discussions on various subjects. While I did not try to give absolutes on the subjects, I did try to encourage the young people by talking about the various pros and cons of many subjects. You might say the discussions were more like my ramblings on where we have been and where we are going as a country. Though I did not give direct answers to where we are going or what should be done, I felt complimented when one of these young people said he thought I was quite intelligent.

One of the things I expressed quite strongly was my feeling about how politicians and the news media view their legislation and stories. I told them that in my opinion, politicians and the news media looked at whatever they were working on at the time with a pair of glasses with two paper cores from toilet paper rolls taped on the lenses. This would help them focus on the specifics of their task without looking at any ideas that might interfere with what they were trying to accomplish. This means that any peripheral problems or negative consequences their actions might cause would not be considered, because they do not want to think about them. They do not want to consider Sir Isaac Newton's third law of physics, "For every action there is an equal but opposite reaction." Yes, politicians and news anchors, these physical laws do apply to legislation and news stories.

This reminds me of the old question, "How do you eat an elephant? One bite at a time." But in doing so, make sure you are not so focused on each bite that you cannot hear the herd sneaking up behind you that is about to stomp all over you. This can apply to being so focused on any problem that you miss the things that can jump up and bite you in the behind.

While working on this book, some have suggested I am trying to cover too broad a range of subject matter. The suggestion was that I should focus on one or two topics instead of the broad number of topics I have included. This is like trying to determine which straw broke the camel's back. If we focus on each individual straw, we can make a good case for why it is there. We can show there is a need for each straw. We have to take a look at the cumulative effect of all the straws to understand why the camel's back was broken. We have to understand that each of the straws, while well intentioned, in combination adds up to an unintended and undesirable consequence. It is these cumulative unintentional and undesirable consequences I am trying to bring to light so we can understand what is happening.

In my young adult years, I remember a puzzle ball that had a large number of round shafts sticking out of it. The object was to try to push all the shafts in. As you pushed in one of the shafts, one or more of the other shafts would move out. As you tried to move another shaft in, another group of shafts would move out. This is not much different than society; as we try to legislate or focus on one problem, another problem will tend to grow. There is no real, absolute solution. The only real answer is to be aware that the problems we try to correct or change will have consequences and make sure these consequences are not worse than the original problem.

Also, in my younger years, there was a game based on making laws. The object of this game was to have each player try to create laws that gave them an advantage and finally to take control of the game. For a game, it was quite exciting to outdo the others and take control, thus rendering your opponents losers. The one advantage to it being a game was that once the game was over, a new game could be started from the beginning, and someone else might have an opportunity to become the winner. In real life, laws become somewhat permanent, and there are only a few winners and many losers. The losers do not have a chance, as they do at the end of the game, to start over from the beginning.

I sometimes wonder what makes me see the broader picture. I have come to the conclusion that I have ADD (Attention Deficit Disorder). I find when reading, studying, listening to or reading the news, or even just watching television, my mind stays active and will jump to topics and ideas that have been triggered by something in what I am trying to focus on.

This may explain why, in my career as a computer software writer, I was able to see how what I was writing would have to be processed by the computer and be able to make it run much faster. This ability helped to save the company I worked for millions of dollars in upgrades to their equipment. As an example, we had a "cost build" (adding all the costs of components and labor to find the cost of a product) that ran eight to nine hours in the overnight run. This caused other morning reports, which had to wait for the cost build to finish, to be delivered to the users late. The head of the department asked me if I could do anything to make this run faster. I told him it might not be easy for the average programmer to follow, but I could probably cut the runtime in half. As this would postpone the need for an expensive upgrade to the computer, I was told to do it. In the end, by not focusing just on the task of doing a cost build but also by looking at how the system had to work to do what I was telling it to do, I was able to take the eight-hour run down to about an hour and forty-five minutes. After that, I was given the task of rewriting the material requirements planning system, which was running about twenty-four hours on the weekend. On this I used the same techniques and was able to take the run down to about six hours.

Since then, new management has decided to change systems. In the process, they brought in vendors to look at our system so they could replace it. Many of the vendors could not understand how we were able to run our cost build and MRP in such a short time. Due to the increase in products, the runtime for the cost build had increased back to about six hours. The vendors thought it should be running twenty-four to thirty-six hours. The MRP was running twelve to fourteen hours and the vendors felt it should be running thirty-six to seventy-two hours.

Why am I dwelling on this? This is an example of not getting so focused on the task that you cannot see what other things are affected. By looking at and understanding how the computer had to process the instructions and realizing there were other ways to do the same thing, I found quicker processes to get the job done.

# What Team Do You Play For?

Are you European American, African American, Mexican American, Asian American, Irish American, Korean American, Polynesian American, Russian American, Chinese American, or Japanese American?

What team do you play for?

The movie *Miracle* illustrates my point. To set the scene, the movie is about a group of hockey players who have been picked from the college ranks to play for the United States in the 1980 Olympics. When they are individually asked who they play for, they respond that they play for the school they were recruited from.

As the story goes, during an international preparation game, the players on the bench were looking around the stands checking out the girls and checking out the some of the opposing players and discussing their strengths. After losing the game, the coach called for some strenuous skating drills. After a session of drills he asked, "Who do you play for?" and someone stated that he played for his college team. The coach called for more drills. At the end he again asked, "Who do you play for?" and the players again said they played for their college teams. This sequence was repeated over and over, with the assistant coach and others questioning the coach's motive and protesting because the players were becoming exhausted. The coach ignored the protestations and called for another sequence of drills. Finally upon the coach asking, "Who do you play for?" one of the players said he played for the United States of America. At this, the coach walked out of the building.

Following this, the team started focusing on the game and started winning games, including the Olympic gold-medal game against Russia. This team was never expected to get to get to the finals. Not only that, they were also expected be massacred if they got that far. Russia was supposed to be unbeatable.

Yes, focusing on the team you are actually affiliated with in sports is very valuable to reaching the goal you are trying to attain. But in sports, the idea is to identify with your team and go out and beat the other team when the game is on. If the players continued this same intense affiliation after the game was over, they would always be trying to be better or fighting any time they met. This would mean the "war" would never be over, and they would not have time to live and enjoy their lives.

In life, we all play for our country. Yes, we are all from different backgrounds and ethnicities, but we are all Americans. Like the players from the different college teams in the movie *Miracle*, we have our own backgrounds, but if we are to win the good life, we must all play for the same team so we all have the same goals.

This is not to say our backgrounds are good or bad or that we should forget where we came from—quite the contrary. We should be proud of our individual heritages. After all, it is diversity that has created this great country.

What happens when we continually press our individual team heritage?

When we press our heritage or views, we open ourselves to other people expressing their heritage or views. This may work well for opening discussion (a game), but to continually press our views is carrying them past the game and does not allow that individual or anyone else time to enjoy life.

People being what they are, they like to categorize things. When they start categorizing, they have a tendency to give qualities (both bad and good) to these categories. People also like to feel they are important by being able to look down on categories they have negative feelings toward.

A current example of this is the Muslims. While many Muslims are very decent people, the few who want to cause trouble are causing the whole of the Muslim people to be categorized as radical. Some people of other groups are taking this categorization as an excuse to attack without regard to whether the person is a radical Muslim or not.

People do not tend to give qualities to people or categories they feel are inferior to them. When they think of Americans, they tend to be proud. When they think of people who live in the same part of the country they live, they tend to be proud—maybe not as proud as they are of Americans, but proud nonetheless. This continues down through the state, city, and community. Other Americans may tend to disagree with what area, state, or city they have pride in. These people are also probably just as proud to be American.

Is it better to focus primarily on what sub-team (city, state, or background) we are, or is it better to focus on the fact that we are all Americans who come from different places or backgrounds? Is it better to focus on what we have in common and can offer or that we come from different places and have different ideas or backgrounds?

Are we Americans of European descent, Americans of African descent, Americans of Asian descent, or Americans of Irish descent? Or better yet, are we just Americans?

America is known as the great melting pot. This is probably because of the blending of the different cultures that arrived on our shores. Many of the people who arrived started picking up different aspects of other cultures. The first thing many immigrants do is to start to learn the English language. One of the first things people start finding in other cultures is food. Then they may start picking up on some of the cultural traditions and ways of doing things.

Even though we are considered the great melting pot, there are many lumps in the pot. We have brown lumps, black lumps, yellow lumps, and white lumps. What do I mean by lumps? Well, we have Mexican Americans. We have Chinese Americans. We have Italian Americans. We have African Americans. We have Korean Americans. We have Japanese Americans. We have Polish Americans. We have American Indians. Oops! How did that happen? Are they Americans first and Indians second? This is an unusual concept. They are Americans first, but they still maintain their Indian heritage.

Why do I consider these lumps? Well, in many of these groups, there are large segments who still speak their own language. For instance, there are many Americans of Mexican descent who have been here for years, and are possibly even American citizens, who still speak only Spanish. I am sure there are parts of areas such as Chinatown or Korea town in our big cities where the inhabitants' native tongue is all that is spoken. This is also true in many of these other groups.

The Americans of African descent are a somewhat different situation. Many of their native languages were lost when they were combined with other Africans and the only common language was English. Currently there is a large group among them that has developed its own words and language. An indication of this separate language is the fact than when people of other ethnic backgrounds use them, American Africans tend to become incensed and offended.

I am an American of German and English descent. I am proud of my heritage. My grandmother and grandfather emigrated from northern Germany. There is a story that has been handed down through my family. One evening at dinner, my grandmother was speaking German. My grandfather, in a heavy German accent, said, "God dammit, Clara, we are in America. Speak English!"

My girlfriend has a similar story. Her grandparents came from Czechoslovakia. Soon after arriving here, the grandfather forbade the speaking of Czechoslovakian in their home.

Many of these early immigrants came here to become part of the great American experience. They wanted to become part of the melting pot. They understood that to do that, they had to leave behind their languages and many of their customs. They realized that to truly become part of America, they had to embrace the American language, laws, and way of doing thing. This did not mean they had to give up their pride in their heritage. They just had to put the way things were done here before their heritage.

They understood it was more important for the country and themselves to blend in to the melting pot. They realized it was important they did not become a lump in the melting pot.

They believed it was more important to play for the American team than to try to bring their individual teams and have everyone going in different directions.

What team do you play for?

Are we focusing too much on our heritage and not focusing on joining the American team and strengthening everyone?

# *Our Founding Fathers*

Our Founding Fathers struggled with large differences of opinion. They worked through these problems to try to establish a constitution that gave the most rights and freedoms to everyone. Even back then, there were factions looking for special considerations and who were able to wield enough political clout to get their agendas included. In the years following the acceptance of the Constitution, most of these agendas have been removed from the Constitution.

The Founding Fathers also gave the right to the people to amend the Constitution. They understood there might be things they missed or that were not evident at the time of the Constitution. They also knew there were things many of them thought should be covered, but the political climate at the time would not allow their inclusion.

But they were also worried about giving these rights. They were worried the people would not have the fortitude to use the right responsibly. They hoped future Americans would use it only to ensure peoples' rights and freedoms and not give rights to one group in favor of another. Responsibility is one thing they could not figure out how to legislate or put into the Constitution.

I do not think these people were politicians but were statesmen. Unfortunately the dictionary definition of statesman does not convey what I want to say. The dictionary definitions I have seen equate politician as a synonym for statesman. A true statesman does not have all the negative baggage that goes with being a politician.

The Founding Fathers were truer statesman. They were more interested in putting together a government that gave rights not to the people but rather to the individual. These were all common men who had an uncommon understanding. They were probably people of various religious beliefs. They also were people who had many ideas of things that were wrong. They all had their own ideas of what was proper or improper for people to do.

These people understood that they as individuals did not have all the answers. They understood that everyone is capable of having good ideas, but if we try to implement all these ideas to all the people, we would not succeed in helping anyone.

These great men realized their individual desires and ideas of how things should be were not the best for all the people. They sat down and decided it was better to focus on the individual's rights. They also realized there was some risk in this idea. They realized there would be some who would want to take advantage of this idea. Their hope was that there would be enough individuals who understood what they were trying to do to be able to keep those who wanted to take advantage in check.

When they crafted the Constitution, they did everything they could to keep personal interests and desires out of the document. They wanted to make sure they did not take any rights away from the individual. They said people had the right to believe in their own religions, even if that religion was not the one the Founding Fathers believed in. There were a few things I am sure that many of them did not want in the Constitution, but because these things were already part of the fabric of the land, they were somewhat forced to include them in order to get a consensus on the document. Most, if not all, of these things were later removed through amendments. Things such as slavery.

Today, as I can see from the dictionary definition, people and politicians do not understand the idea of a statesman. They only understand the idea of a politician. They only think of their pet projects or ideas. They think the government is there to give them a way to impose their ideas on other individuals. They think the common good is better than individual rights. They think what is good for "me" is good for everyone else.

We have hundreds of millions of people who each have an idea of what is good for "me." The vast majority of these ideas seem to have their basis in the same basic idea—that some other individual or individuals should not have the right to their own ideas. People tend to feel that the others' ideas are wrong and that they, themselves, have the only right ideas. These people feel that the other individual's rights are a threat to them and the world as they want to see it.

Unfortunately, I do not see any statesmen among our politicians or leaders. I do not know if this is because being a statesman is a lost art or if it is because so many people are interested in what is good for "me" that they have drowned out those who would be statesmen.

I tend to think it has become a lost art, because with the number of rules and laws we now have, people are feeling that the only way to be able to improve the situation is to create more rules and laws. They feel that to be able to do the things they want, they must be the loudest and strike first before someone else takes more of what they consider their rights away.

I am sure these are the concerns our Founding Fathers had.

The Founding Fathers may have lived hundreds of years ago, when things were quite different from today, but some people would say they were wise beyond their times. I think it is not that they were so much wiser than their times but that they understood the one thing that is constant—people. Times have changed the things we have and use, both for good and bad, have changed but the one thing that hasn't changed is people.

If we look back through time, looking through writings from all the different times, we can see all the same traits of human nature as we see today. So, it is not that we live in a different time; it is only that we have more and different things to use and work with.

The Founding Fathers established how our government was to be structured and established a minimum age for many of the most important positions within the government. I believe this was done to try to ensure that those who filled these positions had some life experiences and would be better able to understand and protect the ideas put forth in the Constitution. Again, they understood the need for responsibility in application of the laws.

Many of the amendments that were added to the Constitution were added to help define responsible applications of the laws. These were added to help prevent irresponsible applications of the fundamental concepts of the Constitution.

The right to free speech was established to prevent anyone or any group from interfering with a person's right to dissent. The Founding Fathers wanted to be sure no one could push an agenda by limiting the ability of others to voice their disagreement. The problem many people have with this amendment is that they cannot accept that someone might say or do something in dissent that they do not like.

One of the current hot-button issues is the burning of the American flag. As long as a person did not steal the flag or cause physical damage to any person or someone else's property, I do not see that it is much different than tearing up a picture of someone. After all, the flag is only a symbol of this great country; it is not the country. This country is not about someone doing or saying something you do not like; it is about embracing the fact that we are all different. We all have different views, and we should embrace the fact that it has been this collection of views that has made us the strong country we are. The one thing that has modified the right to free speech is that you cannot use free speech to injure another person or take away his rights.

In the case of prohibition, an amendment to the Constitution was established to take a freedom away from the people. This amendment caused so many problems and corruption in the country that another amendment had to be passed to repeal it. This is a good example of what our Founding Fathers were trying to achieve. They understood that giving freedom of choice to the people, with all their foibles, was much better than trying to control the people and giving others the opportunity to profit from these controls.

I recently heard a comment on TV that made me think. A person made the comment that the founding fathers did not define the new government as a "democracy." While the dictionary defines a democracy as a government by the people and the founding fathers stated that America was to have a government "of the people, by the people, and for the people," they did not define it as a democracy. Was this an oversight or was it deliberate?

In a democracy, the people have full control over what the laws are to be. If the majority of people want a law and they vote for it, it becomes the rule of the land. This means that if the majority of the people should want to re-institute slavery, this would then become the rule of the land. If the majority of people want to vote to say that the government has full control of the lives of the people, this too would then become the rule of the land.

The Declaration of Independence talks about the fact that a governing body should not be based on "abuses and usurpations" of the rights of any people. This fact is contrary to the one of the fundamentals of a true democracy. As I have shown, in a democracy, if the majority of people, at some time, should decide to pass a law that abuses or usurps the rights of someone or some group, it becomes the law.

In fact, the Constitution starts off with, "We the people of the United States, in order to form a more perfect union ..." It does not state the country was to be governed by the rules of any specific structure of government. All it says is "a more perfect union." The Founding Fathers wanted to leave the structure open to one that would give more rights to the individual than to any group.

The Declaration of Independence says, "That all men are created equal, that they are endowed by their Creator with certain unalienable Rights, that among these are Life, Liberty, and the pursuit of Happiness." This again indicates that the individual is to have more rights than the whole.

It appears the founding fathers were trying to give the all the rights to the individual as long as those rights did not diminish the rights of any other individual or group. This again does not fit with a democracy; in a democracy, if the majority of people want to diminish some individual's or group's rights, they can.

Another indication is that the Constitution calls for a two-thirds vote of both houses or two-thirds of the legislatures to call for a convention consider an amendment. The amendment must be ratified by the legislatures of three-fourths of the states. This indicates that the Founding Fathers wanted considerably more than a 50 percent vote to take any rights away from the people. Today it seems that individual rights are regularly taken away by a simple majority vote. What is happening with our elected officials who are sworn to uphold the Constitution?

I do not think that at the time our founding fathers established our country (nor at present) there was any defined form of government that fit the Founding Fathers' idea of what the government should be or do. Among the many definitions of governments such as democracy, republic, socialism, communism, or any other, they all have one thing in common. They all tend to give control of the individual to some other group. These ideas are not what our founding fathers envisioned. They envisioned a government where the rights of the individual defined the government, not one where the people or the government defined the rights of the individual.

Another interesting fact for those who think America is a democracy is the existence of bureaucracies. These are organizations set up by those who are elected by a majority and then given the authority to create rules or laws that do not have to be voted on. In other words, these bureaucracies have the authority to create laws without regard to what the majority of people want. Therefore the idea of a democracy is defeated by the structures it creates.

It is interesting that all the politicians are saying we are a democracy. They talk about one man one vote. I do not remember voting for a jet engine the military does not want or an off-ramp to increase the value of someone's property or a ship that the navy does not want. I do not remember voting for the red light cameras or mobile radars. I do not remember voting for searches at the airport or wiretaps on my phone. I do not remember voting on giving insurance companies the right to make prescription coverage so confusing. There are lots of things I do not remember having the opportunity to vote on. If this is a democracy, why do the politicians' votes count more than mine does?

It is also interesting how many states try to find ways around the Constitution or just flat out ignore it. The Constitution states there should be no levy on articles moving from one state to another. It also talks about the fact that a citizen "shall be entitled to all privileges of citizens in the several states." This means if a person of one state buys a product in another state, he should not have to pay any entry fee or tax when he returns to his home state.

I have heard of states that want people who have purchased things such as automobiles (on which they have already paid taxes) in another state being charged tax when they returned to their state and registered the vehicle.

Also, I was visiting a friend of mine who lived close to the border of another state. We were driving to the other state when we saw a police officer, for no apparent reason, pull over a car that had just entered the state. I asked my friend what he thought they had done. He told me that cigarettes were heavily taxed in his state and the taxes were less in the other state. He then told me that his state had positioned police officers outside the tobacco store across the line in the other state to see who from their state was buying cigarettes and then radioing back to the officers to stop them when they entered the state. They would then confiscate the cigarettes or collect the tax.

# Politics and Politicians

In order to be able to do anything, politicians must get elected to some position. To get elected, they must be able to focus on convincing voters to vote for them. To get votes, they must be able to convince voters that electing them is in their best interest.

There are several ways this can be done. One is for the politician to know the current hot topic for his constituents. The politician does not necessarily have to agree with what the people want; he only has to focus on the idea and convince them he is sympathetic to their ideas.

Does this mean these ideas are truly the best for the people or the country? Not necessarily! This is one of the downfalls of our current political climate. This should be the time to discuss and educate people on the true pros and cons of an idea. Instead, politicians will either staunchly support or oppose the idea to get the most political gain. One of the reasons for this lack of discussion is that there are so many ideas that must be addressed during a campaign that no single idea can be adequately addressed.

Another way politicians use these hot topics is by taking extreme views in order to polarize the people to their side and show they are in support of one view or the other. This is an attempt to take those who are undecided or moderate and move them to the politician's side.

Another big factor in getting elected is money. Politicians need money to advertise and get their names and views in front of the public. One way to get money is to expand on the above ideas. By polarizing the people, politicians can push some of the people to their more extreme position and get more people to contribute to their campaign. This helps fund more political rhetoric, more polarization, more extreme ideas—and therefore more money.

Is this not a form of corruption? Does this really contribute to the well being of the people and the country? Does this contribute to the support of individual rights? Does this really contribute to constructive discussions of the pros and cons of any idea?

Once elected, a politician needs to focus on reelection. He now has the advantage of "the bully pulpit." This means that because he is in a position of power, he commands the attention of the people and the media. This means his political rhetoric has a sense of fact and importance and is readily disseminated. Thus, he can get his position out without having to pay for it.

Another thing he has is money to use to make the people feel he is doing things for them. He can push things that put his name out there. He can push for projects and expenditures to try to show the people he is doing something good. Are these things truly good or are they good for the politician?

This availability of money to do projects also leaves open the possibility of corruption. Politicians have the ability to use this money for political and personal gain. An example I have heard of was a politician pushing the transportation department to put a "much-needed exit" on the interstate highway. It was later found the politician and some of his friends had recently obtained control of a large amount of property near that exit. This exit would greatly increase the value of the property, thus giving them a large gain. This was all done while the politician was showing his constituents he was doing something for them. I am sure this is not the only example that can be found and that many people are aware of similar situations.

With all of this focus on getting elected, it does not leave much room for true discussion or education on what the people want.

When there is not time to educate, there is time to legislate.

# Political Crimes

What are political crimes? No, I am not talking about crimes committed by politicians. What I am talking about are things defined as crimes that do not result in any loss or damage to anyone. These are often called crimes against the state.

One of the most common political crimes is speeding. Most, if not all, drivers have been guilty of speeding at some time or another. Why do I consider speeding a political crime? Speeding in and of itself is a victimless crime. It then becomes only a crime against the state!

Speed limits are determined by the lesser average. Lawmakers look at how much traffic there is on a road as part of the formula. For example, during the day, if there is a lot of cross traffic, they tend to lower the speed limit. At other times of the day, there may be little or no traffic in the area. At these times, the speed limit could be higher without creating any more danger. So which speed limit is the correct one for the road? Do the police and the photo radar systems take these factors into consideration? No. The speed limit is strictly enforced as a political absolute reality.

I find it interesting that when I am driving and probably going a little faster than the speed limit, I am soundly passed by police cars and other government vehicles. I think we can consider these drivers as professional drivers. Being professional drivers, I am sure they are aware of the road conditions. If these professional drivers feel it is safe to travel well above the posted speed limit, why should we consider the speed limit established by some bureaucrat sitting in some office as being absolute? Who knows better what the safe speed for the area is?

I know many people think and say that speed kills. If this is true, there should be as many deaths as there are occurrences of speeding. The numbers do not support this idea. Some people will say, "Yeah, but speed causes accidents." Again, the numbers do not support this. There is a section of a freeway near where I live where they have put up photo radar cameras that have taken hundreds of speeding pictures per day. If speeding was the cause of accidents, this section of freeway would be littered with so many accidents that it would be impossible to speed or even pass through.

Speed in and of itself is not the problem. It is the people who do other things like obstructing traffic, cutting people off, frequently changing lanes, and other forms of reckless driving that create more danger than speed in and of itself.

Why are politicians and police so focused on speed? Well, that is simple. Speed is something that can be easily defined and measured. This is something that is tailor-made for the police and politicians. This is something that is easy to define and legislate. This means it is easy for the politicians and police to define and generate numbers to show they are proactively doing something "good" for the people. To try to attack the other problems that cause accidents is not so easy. How do you define a law on reckless driving so that a photo radar reckless driving system could be put in place? How do you define a law that punishes someone's slow or obstructive driving that causes others to take chances to get around them, which leads to accidents? This is especially difficult because in cases like this, the persons who actually caused the situation that instigated the accident are often not actually involved in the accident.

Another point on speed is that in hilly areas, the police tend to set up on the downhill slopes. This is where gravity tends to take over and increase the speed of the vehicle. We are in a time where everyone is concerned about fuel efficiency of vehicles. One way to increase fuel efficiency in hilly country is to use the gravity to accelerate your vehicle instead of the engine. This means that while going downhill, your gas mileage increases because you are not using your engine as much. If you have increased your speed because of gravity going downhill, when you start to climb the hill on the other side, you do not have to use your engine as soon to maintain your speed. This means that you do not start using fuel as soon going uphill. But remember, the arbitrary speed limit is more important than saving fuel.

Also, another thing people do not think about is that your brakes use fuel. This is because braking slows your vehicle and to replace that speed, you must use fuel. This is why fuel efficiencies are greater on the open road than around town. In town you are continually speeding up and then using your brakes to get rid of that speed. Each time you have to replace speed that was lost due to braking, you are using extra fuel.

I heard a story from a lady who got a photo radar ticket. She was traveling on a highway and passing some slower traffic. The exit she wanted was coming up, and she was trying to get over to the right. The traffic on the right would not let her in, so she sped up to get in front of the slower traffic and get over to the right. Unfortunately, she came into range of the photo radar camera as she was trying to pass the slower cars. There was not a police officer there to see what was happening, and she received a ticket. As she could not call the camera into court to question it on the situation, she had to pay a hefty fine.

I can understand this problem. I was recently traveling down the interstate with my cruise control on. I was coming down on the car in front of me at a fairly good rate. I did not change my speed, but I moved to the left lane to pass him. As I pulled up beside him, he increased his speed and stayed beside me. I eased down on the gas to complete the pass. With this he also increased his speed and maintained his position on my right. I backed off of the gas to let him move ahead of me. With this he also slowed down and maintained his position on my right. As we were now going slower than I was originally when I started to pass him, I again sped up. He again sped up and maintained his position. At this point, I decided to do whatever it took to get away from this hazard. I continued increasing my speed and at fifteen miles per hour over the speed limit, he was still on my right. Finally at twenty to twenty-five miles per hour over the speed limit, I started to pull away from him, though he stayed fairly close. I maintained this speed until I was considerably past him. Shortly later, I could see that he was starting to slow down. I moved back to the right lane and started to slow down myself. As the distance between us increased, his speed decreased. I finally returned to the speed I was traveling, and he was fairly quickly fading in my rearview mirror.

I feel this is a good example of how someone could be caught by a photo radar system that would not show that there were other circumstances contributing to the speeding. If a police officer had been there, he would have seen that the other driver was obstructing me from safely passing and returning to the right-hand lane.

The government should be doing more to find drivers who obstruct other drivers or interfere with their reasonable use of the road. Slow and inconsiderate drivers are one of the major causes of road rage and probably cause more accidents than just speeding.

Another factor that causes speeding is the setting of speed limits that are not reasonable for the road. Politicians seem to be quick to reduce speeds to bend to constituent pressure. There seem to be many people who think twenty-five miles per hour is too fast. These politicians want to cater to the lowest common denominator.

While politicians are focusing on putting in more photo enforcement, is anyone looking at the legal ramifications? It is my opinion that in the United States we are supposed to be innocent until proven guilty, and we are supposed to be able to question our accuser. With photo enforcement, we are instantly guilty, and there is no opportunity to question the accuser.

My friend, Phil, recently told me a story about his sister. Two cars were in a left turn lane. The light turned green, and they proceeded into the intersection and started their turn. At this time, an elderly person stepped off of the curb on the side road and started crossing the road in front of the lead car. This car stopped to wait for the person to get out of the way. The second car was stopped in the intersection where the sensors were. The light turned red before the cars started moving and the second driver was photographed in the intersection

This person was cited and fined for running a red light. She tried to argue the case before the judge, unsuccessfully. She was denied proper legal protection because she was not able to question the accuser. Had she been ticketed by a police officer, she would have had the opportunity to question the officer about the situation at the time of the ticket

Actually, if there had been a police officer there, he would have seen what had happened, and if he were to give any ticket, it would have been to the person who crossed the road illegally instead of the person(s) trying to avoid an accident.

Here is an interesting thought on red-light cameras. I presume they were put up because of the number of accidents at intersections controlled by red lights. When I was learning to drive, I was taught it was my responsibility to look both ways and make sure it was safe before entering or crossing a highway. This concept also applied to stop signs and stop lights. This makes me wonder if the person who misjudged the time to clear the intersection or the person who just assumed that having the green light meant that he did not have to check for oncoming traffic is responsible for the accident. This is just another indication that politicians do not know how to educate people and opt for the easy answer to make someone else responsible! We pay them to make tough decisions, not to take the easy way out.

As I will discuses elsewhere, there is a concept my father taught me that you can be right and have the right of way but you can also end up "dead right."

Just as a personal aside, when I first saw the "photo enforcement" signs go up in the town I live in, I had a couple of thoughts. First my mind went to the old Soviet Union and the old Germany. These were places where the government had all the control and what they decided to do is the way it would be. They did not care for the average people—they were only something to control. As Mark Twain said, "Nothing so needs reforming as other peoples' habits."

I also find it interesting that politicians are so worried about the many different forms of research that they feel they have to pass laws against them all. These include things like cloning and stem cell research. The reason I find this so interesting is that a number of these research projects hold the potential to help save or make people's lives medically better. No, they are very worried that these projects could be used for other purposes that could be detrimental to society. But it seems that these same politicians have no problem using other research to help them control other people's lives. They do not seem to think that these types of research and the products that are created are harmful to the country or its people. There are probably a couple of reasons for this. One might be that this research helps give them the power over the people, thus fulfilling their need for control. Also, many of these products give them the opportunity to tax or otherwise raise more money from the people to fund their pet projects. It appears that any research that gives them control, power, or money is okay, but those ideas that will help the people and from which they cannot get control or money are not okay.

Secondly, when I saw the photo enforcement sign, I started thinking about how everyone was using acronyms. With this, I was wondering if this was an acronym for something. The one that I came up with is, "Police Helping Organize Totalitarian Oppressive Enforcement."

The following is the text of a ballot proposition I have been thinking about:

Ballot proposition regarding photo enforcement and other media or electronic surveillance.

Any public employee or public official captured breaking any laws by any form of re-playable or permanent surveillance shall be fined or punished, as would any other citizen.

Any public employee or public official found trying to suppress, alter, or ignore such fine or punishment shall be charged with felony interfering with due process punishable by five years in prison and a fifty thousand-dollar fine.

Any supervisory or higher public employee or public official shall be fined at twice the normal fine for these offences.

Any elected public official shall be fined at three times the normal fine for these offences.

These laws are to apply to all public employees, including public safety officers not actually involved in active enforcement or emergency response (i.e., running with lights and sirens).

All incidents so captured and the resulting actions shall be made available to the public in an easy-to-use, web-based research system.

It shall also be a felony, punishable by five years in prison and a fifty thousand-dollar fine, to use any means to disable any surveillance as a means for any public employee or official to avoid surveillance.

All funds raised from fees or fines from any photo or electronic traffic enforcement must be used to fund public driver education. Any existing funding for driver education must be maintained at the same or greater percentage as highest percentage in the two years prior to this enactment.

A board of directors taken from national driver associations to have a broader view should oversee the driver education established. The education should include 30–50 percent instruction and scoring on driver etiquette and courtesies.

# Background

There have been many cases of public employees being involved in accidents or other incidents while not following the rules that would be enforced against the average citizen. Having these laws put in place should reduce such incidents and help save lives.

This would help level the field between government and citizens and return to the constitutional idea that public employees are to be no different than the average citizen.

Supervisory and higher officials make considerably more than many average citizens. This means that a fine to them means they may not have money to go out to dinner, while the same fine to many people may mean that they do not have dinner for several nights or may not be able to pay their rent. This would help even the pain of the fine.

Having national driver associations and/or national highway engineering associations would have a broader view and help keep the education in line with the rest of the country. Also, the funds raised are not to be used to replace currently available funds.

I recently received a newsletter from our town and in it they had a table of the number of traffic tickets issued by the photo enforcement equipment. I presume they were trying to show how great their idea of control is. They talked about how they had issued 1242 tickets in the past month. They also said that the total accidents went from seventy-one to forty-one in the past year. This is over thirty tickets for every one accident they were trying to attribute to this enforcement. This also means they have given tickets to over twelve hundred average people in one month who probably would not have been in an accident.

If this idea is so great, why are will still having accidents? As many experts (especially those in the FAA) have said, accidents are in most cases not the result of only one cause. They are instead a combination of several causes that all came together to cause the accident.

Another interesting thought is that these twelve hundred tickets a month result in fines of between eighteen and twenty-four thousand dollars to the city. That is between two hundred sixteen and two hundred eighty-eight thousand dollars for a year to the city coffers. In a small town, this gives the politicians a lot more money to play with. Are these politicians more interested in our safety and well being or are they more interested in getting their hands on more money?

As for me, I have been doing all my shopping in another town instead of having to run the gauntlet of photo red lights and photo radar between me and the businesses in town. I also know of other people who do not live in the town who, for the same reasons, have reduced or are no longer doing business in the town. Could this reduction in the number of people who are shopping in the town also have contributed to the decrease in traffic accidents?

In talking to some other people in the community, a couple of things have come to light.

The red lights in our area immediately change the cross traffic light to turn green. In other areas and states, the opposing lights are delayed for a couple of seconds to allow someone who might have been caught off guard a chance to clear the intersection before the other traffic starts to move.

A friend told me that the yellow light on one or more of the lights was set about 25 percent shorter than the minimum required for the light. This made it more likely that there would be violations. Of course this would mean more money to the city. Even maintaining the absolute minimum timing on these lights shows the politicians are more interested in collecting fines than in the people they serve or their actual safety.

While I am on red lights, here is something interesting to consider. I do a lot of traveling at many different times of the day and night. One thing I have wondered about is the fact that in off hours, I frequently come up to a red light and have to stop and wait while there is no other traffic in any direction. These red lights were set up to control traffic at an intersection during high traffic times, but have those who decide where these lights should be ever considered lesser or non traffic times? Again, they are only considering the lowest common denominator and in many cases do not consider the impact at other times. Nor do they consider the impact on fuel usage. Or maybe they do—this can generate more gasoline tax.

Another person (a police officer) told me he thought many of the speed limits in and around town were excessively low for the areas and the traffic needs. He also commented that he had worked some of the roads in the hills and mountains around our area. In those areas, they had reduced the speed limits to try to reduce accidents. He said he saw that people became more frustrated and were taking more chances in trying to pass slower cars in short passing areas or even no passing areas. These slower speed limits were in effect causing more road rage.

When I first started driving, seat belts were not standard equipment on cars. I felt they were a good safety idea, and I installed them on my first two cars. Back then, we did not even know what shoulder harnesses were. Seat belts were just the lap belt. Needless to say, I do think they were and are important to my safety.

I also feel it is my choice as to whether I use them. I do not feel the government should be involved in my decision. This is another political crime where the major damage is to the user, not the government. If someone is going to be injured, it is most likely the person who did not use the seat belt, not the government or anyone else. This is a personal choice about personal safety.

People may say that seat belts save lives. This is true, but not everyone who drives will ever have needed a seat belt. In fact, if the statistics were available, they would probably show that more people who have lived and passed on have gone through their lives without ever having needed to be restrained by a seat belt.

This then becomes another example of spinning of numbers and focusing on the smaller number of people who are hurt because of their choice and ignoring the fact that we are taking rights away from the many who probably will never be involved.

Again, this is just another way for governments to take a marginal problem and find a way to take money from people. This is just another example of those who think they know better and have all the "right" answers to impose their will on others. This is just another way for the police to take advantage of a law to flex their muscle by interfering with individual rights.

While I am on the subject of traffic, there is one concept people have that also contributes to many accidents.

This is the concept of "the right of way." Yes, our laws and common courtesies have embedded in them the concept that someone has the right of way. This means that a person by position or timing has the right to proceed and the other persons are to yield the right of way to them. In other words, they are the ones who should proceed while the others should yield to them.

An example might be someone stepping off of the curb and into a crosswalk. This person being in a crosswalk is assumed to have the right of way over the vehicles on the road.

While it is true that this person might have the right of way, there is another concept I would like you to consider. That is "dead right." While this person has the right of way, he should not assume or demand that because he has the right of way he will be safe.

Just because you have the right of way does not mean that someone else will see you or be able to stop in time to keep you safe. All that having the right of way means is that you have a legal right to do something. It does not guarantee that you will be safe. It does not guarantee that you will not be hit or killed. It only means that if your situation ends up in court, you have some legal standing as to being right. It will not bring you back if you are killed because you demanded your right of way. You will still be "dead right."

When exercising your right of way, use some common sense, and do not assume that your life will be protected because you have the right of way. Also, because you think you have the right of way, you do not have the right to put someone else in danger or impose on his rights.

Many political crimes have one thing in common. They tend to presume that someone will be guilty of a crime as opposed to presuming they are innocent until proven guilty of an actual crime. In our society and laws, we are supposed to be innocent until proven guilty.

Another problem with political crimes is that they tend to lead to greed, abuse, and corruption. This phenomenon is starting to show its ugly head in the enforcement of speeding laws. With the use of photo radar and photo red light cameras, politicians are using them to further their careers by expounding on how they are getting tough on crime. They are also finding that by lowering speed limits and keeping yellow lights short, they are able to increase the numbers to make themselves look better. And one final major benefit is that the amounts of money collected from these fines have greatly impacted the funds they can use to make themselves look good. Money is always good for the politician.

I have been talking a lot about driving and laws. One of the problems with driving is that we have replaced education with legislation. I will admit that education will not solve all problems, nor will it eliminate all accidents, but I do not think that legislation has solved or will solve all of these problems either. I also feel that legislation becomes more intrusive into people's lives, gives police and politicians an excuse to get into our lives, and leads to more corruption by giving certain people the ability to break these rules without equal punishment.

When I was learning how to drive, my father did not just teach me how to use the brake, use the clutch (yes, we had clutches), shift gears, and steer. He also taught me how to think about what was happening when I was driving. He didn't teach me hard and fast rules of driving; he taught me to be considerate and what to watch out for. He understood that driving, as well as life, cannot be defined by absolutes. There are always going to be situations that do not fit into absolute rules.

I am going to take some time here to put forth some of the things my father taught me and those I have learned from my own experiences. I am not trying to say that all of these ideas are a cure-all for all of the driving problems, but I think that if people would take these ideas and think about them when they are driving, it would make the experience better for everyone. Even with these ideas, people are still human, and they will make mistakes. A lot of these ideas are ones that will help increase the margin to allow for mistakes and other causes. These ideas can increase the margin between having an accident and having a near miss.

One of the first things my father taught me was that when driving down the road where there are cars parked, always be aware of these cars, because at any time one of them may suddenly pull out in front of you. This one piece of advice has been one of the most important things he taught me. This being aware of parked cars has saved me from many potential accidents. This also applies when I am on the freeway and there are vehicles stopped on the side of the road. If it is possible, I will move to the left away from the stopped vehicle. Then if someone should step out from behind the vehicle or the vehicle should start to enter the lane, I am in a better position and have a little more time to make any necessary corrections to avoid having an accident.

Another thing my father taught me is that I do not own the road. Everyone on the road has an equal right to use the road, and my right to use the road does not give me the right to diminish other people's rights to use and enjoy the road. Not being courteous and not allowing other people to freely use the road can lead to people taking unnecessary chances. This, in other words, can lead to road rage. These people taking unnecessary chances can lead to an accident that could ultimately involve me.

My father taught me that I should not pass on the right; therefore, I should always stay to the right except when passing. This gives someone the chance to pass me properly on the left instead of taking unnecessary chances passing on the right. Also, if someone wants to pass me, I should not do anything to impede their ability to do so. If I am on a two-lane road, I should be aware if they are able to pass safely, and if necessary, I should be ready to slow down so the other car can safely pass and return to the proper lane. Again, it is better to give way instead of forcing the issue, which may result in my being involved in an accident. Also, if I am on a two-lane windy or hilly road that does not allow passing, when I have cars behind me that want to pass, I should find a place to pull off and let them pass.

There are a large number of bigger vehicles such as large trucks and oversized vehicles on the road. While we all have lanes to use, these larger vehicles use a larger portion of their lanes, giving them a smaller margin of error to be able to stay in their lane. I have heard people say that they have their lane, and this is my lane, and they need to stay in theirs. With large vehicles' decreased margin of error in their lane, there is a greater chance that if something happens, they will cross into my lane. With this in mind, I will tend to move over in my lane if possible and give them a little extra room. This gives both of us a little more time to make corrections should they become necessary. This little bit of extra time can make the difference between both of us continuing on safely or my ending up under the wheels of the other vehicle.

On most freeways, the width of the lanes does not change on curves. For longer vehicles, this means the lane actually becomes narrower. This can be demonstrated by drawing a couple of curves like the lane of the road and placing a long ruler between the lines. The longer the ruler or the tighter the curves, the less side-to-side movement it takes to cause part of the ruler to move out of the curves (lane). With this in mind, if I need to pass a long truck on curves, I become aware of how tight the curve is and how narrow the lanes are. If the curves are tight and the lanes are narrow, I will hold off on passing until I reach a straighter section of the road. This again gives me a larger margin for error between safely passing or becoming part of the accident statistics.

A few other things to consider with larger vehicles are that in a contest between a smaller vehicle and a larger vehicle, the smaller vehicle will fare the worse. The tires on trucks are inflated to a much higher pressure and should they for some reason blow, the resulting "explosion" could cause damage or an accident.

With these things in mind, I will do my best to give these vehicles as much room as possible, and when passing them, I will try to get by them as quickly as possible. The longer I am beside them, the more time I am in a position to not be able to react to a problem, and the more likely I am to be involved in an accident.

This also applies with all vehicles. The two things that are very important are time and distance. The more time you spend with smaller distances from other vehicles, the more likely you are to be unable to react quickly enough to get out of a problem. Therefore, the more likely you are to be involved in an accident. This is why people who follow too close for long periods of time or those who stay beside another vehicle for long periods of time are more likely to be in an accident. This also applies to people who tend to obstruct traffic by going slower in traffic or keeping people from passing. They increase their time at lesser distances, giving less time to react to problems and a greater chance for an accident.

Many drivers may feel they have the right to drive the way the do, whether it is driving too slow for the traffic or driving in the left lane, and they may be right, but in too many cases, they can end up "dead right."

# Politicians and Focus

A question that comes to mind is a change in leadership, really a change. In a recent election, one party was able, by a close margin, to take back the majority and thus control from the other party. I know that in this election, I was not completely pleased with what was going on in Washington. This is not to say that I was pleased with the activities of the other party either.

I know many people who are not happy with the political mess in Washington. They are saying, "Who do you vote for? They are all just as bad as each other."

After taking control, these politicians were focusing on the fact that the people wanted a change and because the people voted for them, it meant that the people were approving their agenda.

To me, this change is like taking my red sock off of my right foot and putting it on my left foot and taking my blue sock off of my left foot and putting it on my right foot. Is it the change people are really looking for or is it because the politicians choose to focus on only what they want to see and hear?

I remember there were times during elections when I was growing up that my parents would be discussing candidates and would be deciding not on who to vote for, but who they felt was the lesser of two evils. For me it is not an occasional choice. Deciding which one I disliked more and voting for the other makes most of my choices for candidates.

I do not think I am alone in this. And given this, how can politicians decide that winning an election is a mandate for them to do what they want?

Also, with this trend, why have there not been any candidates who are willing to break away from the political trend and try to do more what is right for the country?

I haven't seen any politicians with the guts to do this since John Kennedy uttered, "Ask not what your country can do for you—ask what you can do for your country."

As we look down from national to state and local politics, we start seeing more focus on trying to please smaller groups of people. One downside to this is that smaller groups tend to become more focused on achieving some goal or another without the benefit of a broader view. These politicians tend to focus on what the people want without concern as to how this fits with what was envisioned by our Founding Fathers.

As these groups get smaller, they tend to be more interested in controlling other people's activities. They see someone doing something in their state, county, or city that they do not like. They do not care if it is legal or protected under the Constitution; they just want to control or change the activity. With all the pressure these groups put on the politicians' need to change the activity, the politicians feel they need to do something. Even if the politician is aware that it is a legal activity, the pressure may push them to find some marginal way try to control the problem.

While I am on this topic, politicians are so focused on gun control, they are making it illegal to carry or possess a gun in certain areas. The problem is that they are allowing police and military to possess and carry guns in these areas. The Constitution states that any law affecting a citizen of the United States must apply to all citizens of the United States. This means that no person should have more rights than any other person.

A quote attributed to Ben Franklin and others states, "He who sacrifices freedom for security deserves neither." Ben and many of the others who have made similar quotes are among those Founding Fathers that helped create our Constitution and thus our country.

This is not an isolated example of the politicians focusing on a political problem and in the process taking rights and freedoms away from the people. I am sure that many readers have example of their own that could be used to further show this trend.

It is interesting that politicians are so very willing to create bureaucracies that have totalitarian structures. They create these bureaucracies with rules that are vague and as a result leave the interpretation of their rules to the individual applying them. This is quite similar to the laws that were developed in Hitler's Germany where they basically said, "If we do not like it, it is against the law." These types of rules or laws might work well if they were being administered by sharp people with strong comprehension and a large dose of common sense. As we all know, not all politicians or bureaucrats are the sharpest tacks in the box. Not only that, but we also open the door for politicians to be able to use these laws to press their agenda. This would not be much different than Hitler and his politicians did with the vague laws they had in Germany.

One group that comes to mind is Child Protective Services (CPS). These people are charged with the task of protecting children. They are given the right to immediately remove children from homes or any other situation that only the person administering the law needs to think is dangerous or unhealthy. Having this power immediately leads to the possibility of the person in that position looking at a situation and seeing what they want to see. At that point in time, they have a totalitarian authority, and what they say goes. There is no question of innocent until proven guilty, and there are no checks and balances as to what is right or wrong. There is only the CPS person making the decision based on how he or she chooses to see the situation.

One story I have heard is that of a mother who spanked her child in a mall. A CPS person was also in the mall and saw the activity and immediately removed the child from the parent's custody. This is all solely based on how that one person thinks others should raise their children. If only one person's opinion is the right one, why are there so many different professional opinions on approaches to raising children? This situation could very well have happened to me. While taking one of my children shopping, he saw something he wanted that I was not prepared to buy for him. At this point, he threw a tantrum in the store. I picked the child up and physically carried him out of the store while he was kicking, screaming, and scratching my arm until it was bleeding. Many people stopped and looked at me like I was killing my child. I am sure that if that CPS person had been there, he would have removed my child from me at that point. He would not have been aware of the precipitating activities or that I was just trying to remove the child from the cause of his tantrum. Yes, I had tried to calm him down before I removed him, but any discussion with him was just adding more fuel to his tantrum.

In either of these cases, is it appropriate for someone to be able to make a judgment on what is happening as a result of something he did not see? Is it appropriate to give someone the absolute ability to remove a child because the parent is trying to discipline or control his or her child in some manner that the CPS worker does not agree with? As we all know, every child is different and responds differently to different forms of discipline. Some children will have their feelings hurt and change their behavior by a disapproving glance while others will take the same glance as a cue to act out more. Every child responds differently to different forms of discipline and just because someone does not particularly approve of one form or other does not necessarily mean that it is not the appropriate action for that child.

Another story I have heard is that of a family that was in a car accident. The paramedics at the scene checked them out and felt they were okay. The father wanted to make sure everyone was okay, so he took them to an emergency room to have everyone checked. Many members of the family were very prone having visible bruising from any minor bump. The staff at the emergency room, seeing the bruising, called CPS. The members of the family were then all placed in separate rooms and grilled about the bruising. This family had just been in a car accident, but that did not seem to matter. They were still humiliated by the overzealous actions of the hospital staff and the CPS officers. They had nothing to go on except for the bruising caused by a car accident, but the family was still considered guilty until the authorities could prove them innocent. The initial fact that they had just come from an accident did not matter. Is the government always right until proven wrong?

Lest you think that I do not think that we should have Child Protective Services, it is quite the contrary. There are many cases where children are in a dangerous situation that they need protection from—situations where they are being sexually abused or where their parents are not able to care for them and there are no other family members immediately able to step in.

CPS is supposed to be there to protect the children from traumatic situations. But we must also remember that removing a child from his home is also a traumatic. In a society where we have politicians passing laws requiring the populace to change their activities to protect the one in a million chance that someone might get injured, how can they justify the fact that these people have the right to take children out of their home without the same protection? Politicians seem to be saying that we must protect everyone from every trauma, but when it comes to the children, we can cause unnecessary trauma to some children to protect the rights of the other children. Just by saying that the CPS officers are required to protect the children based only on their judgment leaves the system open to misuse, abuse, and corruption.

This also starts to point out the double standards that are becoming prevalent in our government. For example, the laws and methods such as red light cameras where people's wrong decisions that must be made in a fraction of a second means that they are guilty of a crime, or because they are not wearing a seat belt, they are guilty of a crime. But when it comes to what politicians want to do, there is not the same standard. If their rules create a one in one thousand chance of injury to someone, it is considered an acceptable risk. Why does a government of the people, by the people, and for the people have more rights to be wrong or do harm than those people that the government is for?

People are also talking about the fact that spanking, abusive behavior, and the like are hereditary and are learned and passed on from our parents. They talk about how breaking the cycle of these things is very difficult. This is also evident in government and politics. We are in a cycle of bullying and control by the government and each generation has watched past generations do it, and they think they too must do it. They have learned it from their parents and their political mentors, and they continue the cycle. This cycle will also be difficult to break unless more of these people start teaching some of the basic principles this country was founded on. This cycle, like that of punishment and abuse in families, will not be broken unless more people start talking about it and teaching other ways of doing things.

As we have seen throughout history, it is always easier to tear down or destroy than it is to create or build.

As I discuss elsewhere in this book, our Founding Fathers gave us a marvelous framework to build a government that was dedicated to the rights of the people. They then left it to the politicians to build on this fundamental framework. Unfortunately, their fears that those who would be left in charge of this framework would not understand its meaning appear to be coming true. It appears that the politicians have become more interested in their ideas and projects than the idea that everyone's individual rights and needs should be their primary objective. They seem to be tearing down this idea to build up their own ideas and egos.

# Political Taxes and Fines

What are political taxes and fines? They are taxes and fines put on us by politicians primarily to control or change human nature or just to support a bureaucracy with marginal impact.

Among these are liquor tax, licensing fees, cigarette taxes, traffic-control fines (especially those mechanically generated), tax on rental units or hotel rooms, and fuel taxes. Why do I include some of these as political taxes? These taxes are a fixed amount that does not take into account the impact on the individual who ultimately has to pay the tax.

I grew up in the forties, fifties, and sixties, and what I remember of the politicians back then is that many of them were looking for ways to line their own pockets. This was not done with the taxes on the people but usually by political favors. Nowadays politicians are still in it for what they can get, but more and more of them are interested in feeding their egos. To do this, they now have to make themselves more popular with the people. They have found that by doing grandiose projects, which may or may not be beneficial, for the people, they can show they are doing great things and get accolades for them. To do these grandiose projects, they need to get their hands on more tax money. They need to raise taxes on the people to show them they are doing things for them. My question is, how many pieces of straw can the camel carry (especially the poorer classes)?

There has been much talk lately about the fact that there is a growing divide between the lower class and the middle and upper classes. (I use the word class in the context of financial class.) People are wondering why the poorer are getting poorer and the rich are getting richer. They are also wondering if there is some conspiracy that is contributing to this.

I do not know if there is a conspiracy or if it is just the ignorance or indifference of politicians and voters who support these types of taxes, among other things.

Let's take a look at a photo red light ticket. It does not take into account the conditions nor if there were any mitigating circumstances. The offender is (in my area) slapped with roughly a $180 fine. This fine is shared with the company installing the red light cameras and the remainder is used for the general fund of the city.

The cost of this ticket to someone in the upper class is really nothing more than a nuisance. This is nothing more than an extremely small amount compared to their net income or net worth. For some, it probably is not as much as they would pay for an average pair of shoes or a small dinner out. Even at that, they would probably not alter any of their activities or purchases because of it.

To someone in the middle class, this is probably the most they would pay for a pair of shoes or an occasional special dinner out. This would have a little sting to them, and they may have to postpone the special pair of shoes or the special night out. This would not be enough to cause them to out and out cancel any of these activities. This group probably includes the politicians who have established the red light cameras and the fines imposed. They do not want to make the fines so severe that they would be hurt by them, but they want to make them large enough to help fill the city coffers.

Now to the lower class. Within this group there is a wide range of financial statuses or capabilities.

There are those who live a very tight, no-frills life and are able to put a little money away for emergencies and possibly with the hope of someday being able to buy a house and move out of the area they live in. This fine to them would probably set them back months on what they are able to put away. Or it might cause them to postpone the replacing of their children's shoes that are starting to look ratty or have holes in them. It may cause them to cancel taking their kids to the pizza parlor for several months.

There are those who are living a very tight, no-frills life just to stay afloat. For them these fines would mean that they would have to postpone buying shoes for their family for many months. That fine could be their budget for taking the kids out for pizza or meals for a year. It may mean that they will skip lunches to cover the fine.

There are those who are living an extremely tight, no-frills life and depending on help from the outside to help feed and clothe their children. They have a car so they can get back and forth to work so they can earn the little bit they make. To them this ticket might mean missing a car payment and losing their job. It may mean that their rent does not get paid and the risk of losing their home. This ticket may mean that there is no food in the house and the children go hungry.

I feel these are political taxes and fines because it is one that helps further separate those in the lower class from those above them. It is a way to keep this class from achieving a higher status. It is a way for some companies to line their pockets and politicians to get their hands on more money for their pet projects.

Also, the more people are in need of help and the more help they need, the more opportunity politicians have to convince them they are trying to help them and convince them to vote for them.

# Spinning the Numbers

While we all know that politicians put a spin on things to make themselves look better, they are not the only ones that are doing it. The media is also quite guilty of spinning stories to make them more exciting or to push their own agenda.

An example I remember has to do with reducing traffic. Those who were pressing for carpooling were saying that if everyone carpooled to and from work, it would cut the number of cars on the road by half. A study out at the time said that over half of the cars on the road were running errands or just traveling. So if more than half of the cars on the road are not just going to or from work, how can workers carpooling cut the number of cars on the road in half?

One large spin coming out of the political arena is the spin on the national debt. The national debt is now one of the biggest targets for presidential candidates to make predictions and promises about. People are focused on the belief that this is the amount that we as a country owe. If I am not mistaken, somewhere back in the eighties or nineties, Congress was able to create a different category of borrowing that is not included in the "national debt." If this is true, first, the national debt is not the total debt owed by the government, and second, this makes it much easier to manipulate the debt for political gain.

By keeping the focus on the national debt, the politicians know they have something that they can use for political advantage. Somewhere back in the fifties or sixties there was an article in *Playboy* that I believe was written by J. Paul Getty. In this article, he discussed the national debt and how it is reported by the government as opposed to how it would be reported by a business. One of the major differences he discussed is that in business, this would be reported on a balance sheet. This balance sheet would also list all of the assets of the business.

For the government, these would be things like national park lands, governmental buildings, vehicles, military property and equipment, the national highway system, and property and equipment belonging to the many departments within the government. If all this were listed, the amount of the debt compared to the total assets would not be as daunting a number. It is possible that the value of the assets could possibly be greater than the reported debt.

He also commented on the fact that if business kept their books the way the government does, those running these businesses would probably be thrust into jail.

Have you noticed that when politicians are talking about how much money they are going to save, they talk in dollars saved over ten or twenty years? This makes the savings sound so much greater. When they talk about costs of something, they will tend to talk about cost for months or a year to help make the cost sound less. Another advantage of this apples and oranges approach is that it is harder to figure out what the net effect is and how it will affect the overall budget and/or debt.

Another big spin number that politicians and the media love to attack is when they talk about how some company has, for example, a 2,000 percent increase in their income. This does not indicate whether the profits were reasonable. This is just a way to make the numbers sound more exciting to generate more interest in the story. Another form of this is just reporting the huge dollar amount of their income, which again does not indicate whether these returns are bad, reasonable, or excessive. This is usually done with companies that tend to be easy targets like oil or chemical companies.

Let's look at a 2,000 percent increase in income. Let's say you invest one thousand dollars in the stock market. This year the market does not do well and you end up with only a five-dollar gain. The next year the market does better and you make a one hundred-dollar profit. This is only a 10 percent return on your investment for the year, but you have a 2,000 percent increase in your income. Also, if you combine your return for the two years, you have a one hundred and five-dollar return, which is only a 5.25 percent simple return on your money. If you had invested your money a year earlier and had only broken even in that year, the three-year simple return would have only been 3.5 percent (not a great return). I do not know what that 2,000 percent increase in profits really means, but I do know that that percentage is not really a decent indicator of what actual return the company is getting. I cannot make a judgment as to the reasonableness of the return. All I can say is by using these numbers, politicians are able to get many people to think that the target company is bad, and that the company is basically stealing from the people whether it is true or not.

Gasoline prices have been in the news lately. The media says that even with inflation, the price of gasoline is now the highest it has ever been. The questions is, who is spinning the numbers, and are they real?

Yes, the price of oil is up but not as much as the price of gasoline. There are many factors involved in these numbers. Many of these factors are overlooked or not understood by the masses.

Let's look at the fact that many refineries shut down at the same time. People think this is a conspiracy, but from what I know, there is a reasonable explanation for this. One of the reasons I have heard is that during the wintertime, the refineries are changed to produce more heating oil and less gasoline. This means that sometime in the fall, most, if not all, refineries must shut down to make the necessary changes to alter this ratio. Then again in the springtime, they have to shut down to make the changes so that they get more gasoline per barrel and less heating oil. Also included in this is the production of the various grades of diesel fuel, aviation fuel, and other products.

Usually during these shutdowns, they do the necessary maintenance or upgrades to the systems. Some people use this fact to spin the idea that the oil companies are all deliberately shutting down for maintenance at the same time just to drive up prices.

During these times of shutdown, the amount of gasoline and other products available is reduced, and therefore the rules of supply and demand start to take effect. This means that the price for these products goes up.

Just adjusting the percentages is not the only reason for the shutdowns and conversions to take place. Many, if not all, areas of the country require a change in the formulation of gasoline for the summer months. This also requires changes to the process and a shutdown of the processing plants.

Because of this requirement to have certain formulation changes in effect on a certain date, all refineries have to make the changes in as short of a window as possible. This window for making the change is the same for all refineries, so they all must be done at roughly the same time. This means that there is little flexibility in when these changes are made and therefore a greater impact on available supply.

If, during this time of conversions, any of the processing plants in operation should have a fire or other problem that causes an unscheduled shutdown, this will also decrease the available supply. Again, this decrease will affect the law of supply and demand and drive up the price.

For those in California, the problem is increased. The government there has made formulation requirements that are unique to them. From what I understand, this formulation is more expensive to produce.

I understand that this special formulation is supposed to cut emissions by about 10 percent. I had a car that I was able to go over 550 miles on a tank of gasoline. When I filled up in California and drove 495 miles, the low level light on my gas tank came on. This would appear to mean I was getting about 10 percent less mileage on that gasoline. This makes me wonder if the 10 percent more fuel I was using was not offsetting the spin number of 10 percent reduction in emissions. Also, this tells me that when in some states the price of gasoline is around $3.00 and the California prices are around $3.60, the actual price I would be paying is more like $4.00 to drive the same distance.

The other problem with California's special blend is that it is not used in any of the neighboring states. This means that oil companies cannot import oil from any of these states. Without this ability, they must rely only on their own refineries. This again reduces the available supply and, by the laws of supply and demand, creates higher prices.

The federal government is now conducting hearings into why the cost of gasoline is so high. I think if we look at the problem, we will notice that the government is one of the problems. First, they require all the refineries to convert to the summer and winter blends at the same time. Second, as we have said, the state of California requires a more-expensive blend and one that is only available from California refineries.

Another major problem is all the government requirements and regulations on refineries and their construction. Because of all the various laws, regulations, and bureaucracies involved, we have not had a new refinery built in something like twenty-five years. There is currently a large refinery being planed for the Yuma, Arizona, area. From what I understand, it will be five or more years before they can satisfy all the legal requirements so they can start working on the construction.

All of this time is costing the company trying to build this refinery a lot of money. This cost will eventually be built into the cost of the gasoline. With this in mind, why does the government, who is questioning the cost of gasoline, not look inward and try to do something about this problem?

I am not saying we should just ignore the requirements of safety and the environment. But it seems that the government should take a look at all the different bureaucracies, regulatory districts, and state and local fiefdoms that have various ideas about how things need to be done. The government should either force all of them to use the same rules or to set up an agency that is one point for large projects like these to go to. This agency should only require one application and then it would be able resolve the requirements and their variations throughout all the different controlling districts. This should all be done in a timely manner. I feel that the sooner that this new refinery is put online, the sooner the supply of gasoline would go up and the law of supply and demand would help reduce the price of the products.

One other way to reduce the price of gasoline is to impose rationing. This has been tried many times on many products. In most of these attempts, one of the biggest problems is corruption. People found ways to make money by helping people get around these laws.

Here again the law of supply and demand is probably the best answer. The increase in price causes usage to go down. The reduction in demand starts reducing price. A problem that occurred when we had even/odd day rationing was that many people's businesses required lots of driving, and they needed gasoline on a daily basis. The rationing caused many of them to not work on days they could not get gasoline. This then started causing problems with the gross national product and started sending us toward a recession.

Another thing that is a spin on numbers is the problem with Social Security. Yes, there is probably a problem with the solvency of Social Security. But I find it interesting that the government has made Social Security benefits taxable. This does a couple of things. First, this means the benefit some people receive is reduced and to help offset this and keep them from falling further below the property level, the benefits will eventually need to be increased. Second, the taxes collected from Social Security that were to be used to help people can now be diverted so that politicians can use it. As an idea, if taxes are collected from anyone receiving Social Security benefits, these taxes should be put back into the Social Security fund. This could help prolong the solvency of the Social Security fund with money that was from the fund in the first place instead of letting the politicians divert it.

Let's look at another way that the dollars can be spun. As an example, and not to be pro- or anti-war, let's look at some of the costs of the war. This can also apply to other things, but when we are figuring the dollar cost of deploying troops, are we including in these numbers the cost that would have been there to have them at home? That is, if these troops were at home, they would be receiving their pay and we would be paying for housing and training for them. Having them off fighting the war (or down in New Orleans) does have a cost, but is what we are reporting as the cost the incremental cost over and above what would have been the ongoing cost, or is this including these base costs? For those yelling about the costs, I am sure they would want to inflate the cost and not report it as just the incremental cost. I am sure there are other places in the government that the methods could and are being used.

One interesting thing is that there is only one place the federal government spends money. That is defense spending. They do not spend money on anything else. That is all done by an appropriation! How's that for spin?

I find there are a large number of average people who are grieving over some injury or death that has tragically occurred in their lives. They will take some unusual incident, failure, or accident that has caused this tragedy and run to a TV station and start inciting people into believing the masses must do something to prevent this from happening again. While many of these may and do deserve some attention, those pressing for action are not just interested in just making people aware of the problem. They are also using their grief to press for an absolute zero probability of this ever happening again. Many times they will use the fact that a child was involved to try to increase the emotional factor.

These people are not interested in how the changes they want will affect other people or the total cost of their ideas. They do not take a look at the perspective of their incident as a percentage of the total number of potential times the incident could occur. Many of these problems are one in one hundred million potential occurrences or greater. This means that the problem does not occur 99.999999 percent of the time.

If we required this type of error percentage in most of the things that we take for granted, we would be surprised to realize how many things we now take for granted would not meet this standard.

Let's take a look at medicines and medical procedures, for example. If these types of percentages for not having any negative effect were imposed, I do not think any medical procedure or prescription medicine would be allowed. Also, most over-the-counter medicines would be gone. There are many people who cannot take things such as aspirin, and this would push its safety factor above this percentage. When you take into consideration that there are potential problems with drug interaction, all medicines would not be able to meet these standards.

Now let's look at food in general. There are enough people who are highly allergic to peanuts or peanut butter that this would also not meet this standard. If you do not think peanut butter is dangerous, just consider the fact that there was a story of a man who had a peanut butter sandwich on an airplane going to visit his girlfriend. When he got to his destination, he kissed his girlfriend and a short time later she died from an allergy to the peanut butter.

Many people have allergies to nuts and other foods. I, and some other members of my family, have some allergic reactions to different types of cheese. I personally have to be careful as to what cheeses are being used in cooking. I do not have to eat the cheese. I just have to be near where it is being cooked.

Given all this, is it really in the best interest of the country that we should have a knee-jerk reaction every time someone does something stupid that causes an injury or death? Should we turn businesses and industries upside down to prevent that one in a billion occurrence when the change itself might create other possibilities that themselves might not meet the requirements because no one could foresee a potential problem?

# The Media

As with politicians, the media needs to get the people to believe they are in their corner in order to get them to subscribe to their services. To do this, they must also focus on the hot topics. Unlike politicians, the media will tend to take the most popular view of the topic to appeal to the most people. To underline this focus on mass appeal, a commentator on ABC TV was defending the media and their supposed bias by stating that they were covering the news that lay between the forty-yard lines. This is a reference to the center part of a football field. This means that if they were actually covering a football game, they would never be able to cover any scoring.

This means they must focus through their colored glasses and toilet paper tubes to make sure they stay on the popular view.

Why does it seem that those who have the most limited or narrowest views seem to be the most vocal and most able to get public and media attention? It appears that the narrower the view, the more attention and conversely the broader the view, the less the media attention.

When I was growing up, I often heard of the media being referred to as "the fourth estate." This was a reference to the three main branches of government and the media's position as a watchdog over them. Having the attention of the public, they could focus on the flaws and foibles of the politicians and their legislation. They also had the opportunity to educate the people. They were, by their unique position, expected not only to report on the legislative goings on, but they were also expected to do an analysis of the pros and cons of what the politicians were doing.

These days it seems that the media is only interested in the popular view, which is, most of the time, what the politicians are saying. This only makes sense, because the politicians were elected in a popular vote. But does this mean that the popular view is the best view? Is the media trying to so hard to please everyone that they please no one?

Prohibition was passed because it was the popular view of the time, but as it was being pressed on the people, many other problems arose from its enforcement. The problems and corruption became so rampant that prohibition had to be repealed. In this case, reporting between the forty-yard lines and focusing only on the popular view of the problem let the people down and led to a violent time in our history.

With this in mind, is it in the best interest of the people for the media to focus on sound bites of the popular or political view, or should they be including some education on the meaning of the sound bites? Of course this would mean that they would have to get out of their comfort zone between the forty-yard lines.

Many things that are being pressed by the politicians and popular views have constitutional implications. Many of these views are contrary to the things that have made this country great. Yet the media reports them as if there is no downside and basically supports the popular view without question. This far from what a true fourth estate would do.

All of this is coming from the same media that when reporting on an accident or shooting will go up to the wife, husband, mother, or father of the victim and ask, "How are you feeling about this loss?" Do they feel there is some great insight that is going to change the outcome for the better? They are willing focus on the fact that something bad has happened and to ask these kinds of questions after the damage has occurred. But when it comes to political or popular topics, they are not willing to ask what the unexpected consequences of the view might be.

The media is allowing the use of children to further their and others' profits. Children's minds and thought processes are still in the development stages. Their minds are still developing the connections that gives them the ability to understand and make reasonable choices. They do not fully have the ability to understand what is right or wrong or what is good or bad. In fact, I have heard that the brain does not fully develop all of these abilities until people reach their early twenties. In other words, we do not completely develop these concepts of good and bad, right or wrong, until then.

This can be seen in the many stages of a child's development. Young children do not understand the concept of hot or cold. A young child may see a hot burner on a stove and decide to go over and put his hand on it. As the child gets older, he will probably understand this but may not understand that it is dangerous to run into the street. This is all the progression of the brain processing and understanding the world around him. As I have said, children's understanding of their wants and needs, good or bad, right or wrong, do not fully develop until the early twenties.

The media is including or allowing the placement of advertising in their shows and stories that are directed at children. They are taking things that should be nothing more than entertainment or education directed at children and using it to convince children they need to buy certain products. They are using the fact that the minds of these children are not developed to get them to think the way they want them to and to buy the products they want them to.

Another thing they are doing is to have children doing commercials where they are making statements on how they think other people, especially adults, should act or even vote. These are children who have not developed the cognitive power to understand what it really is they are doing or saying. These are children who may be being coerced into saying or doing things that later in life they would not agree with. These are children who are trying to tell me I should vote for someone or something but they have not fully developed the understanding of the dangers of running into the street. These are children who are so focused on chasing a ball that they are unaware of the cars that may be coming down on them.

Just remember that it is because these younger people have not fully developed these skills that it makes them so susceptible to joining gangs or other radical groups. These types of groups depend on this fact to mold or convince these younger people they have the best ideas. That is why in many developing countries the radical groups are teaching these children, even preteens, to take weapons and go out and fight their battles. These radical groups understand that they need to mold children before they develop their cognitive skills to fully understand the right and wrong of what they are doing.

Is the media moving toward a slippery slope? Recently on one of the local channels, I observed a report on where paroled convicts were living in the community. As I was listening to this, I was wondering if the media were not setting themselves up as judge and jury. Also I was thinking, does this not breed hatred and distrust? Does the world need more hatred and distrust?

While these people were convicted of a crime, I do not feel it is the job of the media to keep focusing a spotlight on these people.

These people were caught and then tried and convicted in accordance with our laws. These laws specify a punishment for their actions. These people have served their time and are possibly still serving under the probation provisions. So these people have paid their debt (or are still paying their debt) to society. This debt was established by society as being appropriate for the crime.

Is this any different than paying a parking ticket? Once you have paid your parking ticket, you have met your obligation and should not have to be retried in the media. After you have paid your debt, should you have to be placed in front of your neighbors as a "criminal" for them to pass further judgment on you?

Our laws and their punishments are supposed to be appropriate for the crime. They are designed to try to be severe enough to be a wake-up call to the person. With this wake-up call, there is a hope that the person will try to reform his ways.

These criminals have completed their jail time and are now are back in the general public. They will need to find a place to live and work to support themselves. While a number of them will not be able to make this transition, others may have learned their lesson and want to get on with their lives.

How can we expect these people to be able to turn away from crime if they are continually being put in the spotlight by the media? If they are looking for a job, how many businesses would be willing to hire them if the media is continually pointing them out? These businesses will be worried that many people who see them will not want to do business with them because of the mistake their employee made. It is the same with housing. Many places will decide they do not want to rent to them because of the media attention.

Without the opportunity to find work or a place to live, what is left for these people to do? So, because of the media's judging that all of these people will continue to be criminals and deserve continued punishment and harassment, they are guaranteeing they will not be able to reform.

This then becomes what is called a self-fulfilling prophecy, and the media's idea that all of these people will continue to be criminals becomes true.

What is next? Will the media keep stirring up the public to the point that we, like other societies, require that everyone who has been convicted of a crime have their ID tattooed across their foreheads?

Is it the job of the media to turn people against any other group of people? Is it the job of the media to guarantee that criminals should not have a reasonable opportunity to put their criminal activity behind them? Is it the job of the media to mete out more punishment than the courts and laws have determined reasonable?

As a follow-up on this subject, the media during this report had an expert say that of the group of people they were talking about, about 25 percent of them would return to crime. The expert said about 75 percent of these people will have learned their lesson and return to being a good citizens. This means that the media is continuing to punish the 75 percent and possibly making it impossible for some of these people to return to a good-citizen status.

Why does the media not cover other stories with the same zeal. I am sure the media will say that they have a special page or show that covers many of the stories in more detail. While this is true, there are several problems with this. Many times these editorials will take on a pure support or pure opposition stance. The larger problem is that not everyone who hears something on the news will seek out a special that covers the topic. The only way many people hear about the topic is the actual news presentation, and in most cases they take it at face value. Like the reporter who asks the grieving relative how he or she feels, the reporters of political or popular views should also ask what the negative or unwanted side effects are.

Along with reporting the pros and cons, it would be nice to see some reporting on the historical world and what the outcomes from prior attempts were.

In other words, the media should not be so focused on the story that they fail to report on the story.

These might be some of the reasons that several people I know say they will no longer watch the news, and why I tend not to read newspapers. Could this be why circulation is sagging for many newspapers?

As for the national network news, it appears they are having such a problem reporting political news that they are now more interested and do more reporting on health issues. Not only do they do more reporting on health, but they also do more in-depth reporting on that than anything else. One thing they don't report on is if the source of the information is coming from an organization that supports legislation to further their ideas and control the people.

I have just realized an interesting similarity between news media and politics. Recently on CBS news, Katie Couric became the first female news anchor on TV. This generated a lot of interest, and her ratings started off extremely high. This is very similar to what is happening in politics in that people are looking for a change. As people have found there is not much change in the reporting other than a new set and that it is a female doing the reporting, the ratings have dropped considerably. The media is missing the point the same way politicians are. People are looking for people who are going to help improve their lives, not for people who are just reiterating the idea that it is better if the government controls everyone's lives. Couric had a great opportunity to take the media back to the basics of journalism and challenge our leaders on their ideas of controlling the people and taking more control of all parts of our lives and work. Instead she opted to become yet another outlet for the political line. Just because more than 50 percent of the people think an idea is great does not mean it is. In many cases this majority is created because our media outlets fail to fully report on the idea and its downsides. They fail to challenge the idea and those who are pushing it.

Again, people are looking for change. I do not think that moving the red sock from their right foot to the left and moving the blue sock from their left foot to the right is the type of change people are looking for. Change in leadership or personality is not a change. These people need to step back and look at the basics. They need to take a hard look at the fundamental principles and see if they have been lost in the rhetoric—to see if they have not gotten too involved trying to look like they are doing the job that they are failing to do the job.

If people started doing their jobs, the general public would sit up and take notice. People have become so numbed by what is going on in general that someone actually doing their job would stand out.

Many media outlets say that they are investigative. Some of the most successful TV series of this time are the *CSI* programs and the *Law and Order* series. The basic ideas of these programs are to show all the different investigative techniques that are used to solve crimes.

Many people attribute the success of these programs to the fact that people are interested in seeing and understanding how people go about investigating crimes. They become fascinated with the many different aspects of the investigations and all the various ways they use to develop the evidence. They do not just find the murder weapon and focus on it as the only evidence and try to build the whole case on it. They look at the entire crime scene and try to find other pieces of evidence that may be pertinent to the case. They often find some small detail such as a hair or fiber that may be a link in the case. This is usually something that is much smaller and less obvious than the item that was used to commit the crime.

Quite often, the evidence collected in the first look at the crime scene does not completely solve the crime, but it may give clues to other things that may still be at the crime scene. These folks frequently return to the crime scene to look for things they may have missed in the first pass, but due to other things they have found, they may have a different idea of things to look for.

These people do not just rely on an initial report of the crime where someone says they know who committed the crime and how they did it. They look at all the evidence they can find and see if all the pieces fit.

Even with the in-depth studying of the evidence, they can still come up with the wrong conclusion. But with this in-depth investigation, the number of correct answers goes up while the number of incorrect answers goes down. In other words, they get more of the right answers, and they are not blinded by someone's idea of what the right answer should be.

Most, if not all, TV news shows I have watched say they are investigative. My My *Random House College Dictionary* defines investigate as, "To observe or inquire into in detail; examine systematically." Given the fact that many of the stories are as is and fact, I do not understand how they can say that they are investigative. They take stories from other sources and do no more than pass them on.

They never question anything that is being said in the story. In other words, they take the initial report where someone says they know who committed the crime and treat that as being the absolute correct answer.

The media seems to be happy to report that our representatives are passing laws to control our lives without ever investigating the possible ramifications of these laws. Where is the investigative part of these reports?

They report what organizations such as the American Cancer Society or the American Lung Associations want the people to hear to further their ideas and control. Where is the investigative part of these stories?

What do these media outlets consider to be investigative? Is it that they spent some time going through all the available stories that others have sent them and decide which ones fit their ideas? Is it that they select stories that will fill a given amount of time or space? Is it that they select a story because they feel that they can present it and not have to do any investigating on their own? Is it that if these stories come from a nationally known source, they think that the source is going to discuss anything that is contrary to what their objective is?

As you should be able to see from my writings, everything dealing with political or social topics has many different aspects. All of these types of stories have plenty of opportunities for investigation. Of course, investigating these types of stories might cause the reporters to rethink some of their own ideas and stands on these topics.

All of this makes me wonder if these reporters don't care about getting it right or are they too lazy to investigate the story or are they deliberately not investigating so that they can further their own ideas and agendas?

Recently two TV reporters were working on the same news story. During a break, the microphones were still open and one of the reporters was heard discussing the fact that the other reporter was getting more airtime. This leaves me to wonder if all the reporters are not more interested in airtime or printed lines than they are in the story they are reporting.

In the interest of fairness and the fact that I am somewhat accusing reporters and other media of trying to push their agenda, I think I should tell you what my agenda is for this book.

For me, the reason for this book (which is another form of the media) is not to try to tell people how to act or live their lives. The main agenda is to try to get people to look past what people are trying to tell them to do.

I want people to think about what people are saying. Do not accept that you are being told that there is only an up side to what people are telling you to do.

Take a critical look at what is being said as well as what is not being said. There is usually more that you are not being told than what is actually being said.

People say that the world has changed. I agree; the world has changed. We have more and different things to use, and we have more access to these things.

One thing that has not changed is people. People have the same needs and desires that they have had since the beginning of recorded history. There are still good and bad people. There are still people who want to control other people. But I still think that the majority of people are good people who want to live their lives with a minimum of interference from others. I also have faith that if these people are made aware of all of the facts, they will make the best decisions for themselves and allow others to make their own decisions.

I think this is the idea and structure that our Founding Fathers had in mind when they established this country.

# The Attack on Tobacco

An attack on tobacco is currently being heavily pushed in the media, legislation, and in the courts. One thing I want to make clear is that I am not trying to say that smoking is great or is not a health risk. But I do feel that it is a good example of how focusing and trying to get everyone else focused on a problem blinds everyone to the other negative effects that it may be causing.

Let's look at some historical background. Ever since the beginning of recorded history, people have looked for ways to ease the difficult task that is living. They have found some form of "narcotic" to help them feel better and get though the difficulties. While they may not have been what we now define as a narcotic, they were "pleasures" that helped ease the mind and make life more bearable. Because of the pleasurable effect of these "narcotics," people tend to keep returning to them over and over.

Here is a story I heard about a scientific study. A group of mice were given two dishes, one with water and the other with alcohol. After a period of time, the researchers found that the percentage of those mice that did not drink the alcohol was very similar to the percentage of people where "teetotalers." The percentage of those mice that used the alcohol moderately was also about the same as that of the general population. And those mice that turned heavily to the alcohol were again the same as the percentage of the general population.

This indicates that the desire for alcohol or other narcotics is something that is more desired in some areas of the population than other areas of the population. It also indicates that those who do not have the desire should be less judgmental of those who do.

Let's look at more recent history. In the early twentieth century, a group tried to get rid of another "narcotic"—alcohol. They too did not consider the consequences of what they were doing other than they were trying to get rid of what they perceived as a danger to the people. They were making great strides in ridding the country of the problem. They even were able to get the eighteenth amendment to the Constitution making alcohol illegal. The people were still looking for something to help them get through life. There were not too many alternatives readily available, and many people saw an opportunity. Moonshine (which had been around in small areas of the country) grew in popularity. Others saw an opportunity and started smuggling liquor from outside the country. This led to large organizations of criminals who profited from these activities. These organizations then became quite strong and were able to buy public officials and police so they could conduct their business without interference. When they saturated their territories, they started to move into other organizations' territories. This then led to fighting among the organizations.

All this led to more alcoholics and problems than there were before. Finally the people were able to recognize that in trying to rid themselves of this problem, they had not only made the problem worse but also had created many other problems in the process. They realized they could not get rid of this "narcotic" and all they could really do was to try to minimize its effect. This realization led to the twenty-first amendment to the Constitution repealing the prohibition of alcohol.

Something interesting I recently heard on the news is that women's groups are among the major proponents of banning tobacco. I find this interesting, because women's groups such as the suffragettes and the temperance movement were the main driving forces during prohibition. Is there something missing in women's education such that they do not learn from history?

Maybe this is an indication of why women are so good at mothering. Bringing up young children requires a person to make many decisions about what the child should or should not do for his own protection. Young children have not yet developed the ability to fully understand all the situations they encounter and therefore need someone to tell them right from wrong or warn them about dangerous situations. This may also be an indication of why mothers and older daughters tend to have an adversarial relationship. They both want to be the one telling the other what they think should be done.

A recent TV show I watched was one where a mother was still continually telling her adult daughter how to dress and that she needed to lose weight. This had been going on since the woman was a child. One thing that was brought out was that the mother was doing this out of love for her daughter. Another thing that was brought out was the fact that the mother's continual urging of her daughter to lose weight had caused her daughter to take the extra helpings or desserts just to exhibit the fact that she had her own life. This rebellion against the constant attempts at control was shown to be one of the major reasons for the daughter's weight problem. It was determined that the mother needed to back off trying to control her daughter's life and let her become her own adult.

I am not trying to be negative toward women. It is well-known that there are feminine and masculine traits. Men are known as hunters and protectors, and women are known to be gatherers. Women are known for their love of shopping while men tend to go to the store to get something specific. As with men and their protective nature, realizing that direct confrontation is not always the best way, I feel that women need to start finding other ways of achieving their goals without being as direct as setting laws and rules. The overly protective and controlling method may be subtler than the confrontational method of men, but in my opinion it is no less damaging to the other person. Again, we might consider education over legislation.

I find these facts interesting in that the women in this country are so against the government telling them what they can and cannot do with their bodies with regard to issues like abortion, but they seem willing to try to have the government tell other people what they can or cannot do.

Given this, I also wonder if this might also be part of the cause of the problems that women are having in getting ahead in the business world. Are they approaching that task the same as they approach child rearing? They say they have been successful at running the household for many years, so they should be able to run a business. They need to understand that there is a difference between controlling the behavior of an adolescent and controlling the actions of adults in a business.

To everyone, the reason for this book is to try to get people to think about what they are doing. In the same way that many people think they sound good when they are singing in the shower and find out they do not sound so good when they are recorded, just because we think that an idea sounds good does not mean it is good when applied to everyone.

As we see from the above, when we try to control things, we leave open the opportunity for greed and corruption, and we usually make the problem worse. I feel this also applies to the current push against tobacco.

Let us start by looking at the lawsuits that were brought against the tobacco companies. The attorney generals of many states got together and worked hard to win a large settlement that was to be used for tobacco-related issues. Now that we are several years down from that settlement, we can see that now that the politicians have gotten their hands on the money, it is being used more for other things like roads and such. This, in effect, is buying the support for the politicians who are able to use the money to make them look good to their constituents.

These high-dollar lawsuits have also affected the cost of health care and other products. This is because all of these lawsuits and exorbitant awards have forced companies and providers to pay higher insurance rates because of the precedence of the large penalties. These large penalties are being carried on to other damage suits.

They have also had the effect of when the lawyers are going for the big penalties, they are not just talking about the injury to the persons involved in the suit. They are telling the juries about all the other people they feel have been injured. This means that the companies and their insurers may be paying penalties multiple times as each case is including people they have already paid penalties to or for. In fairness, the Supreme Court has recently ruled on the ability of lawyers to ask for penalties for people not included directly in the lawsuit.

Another thing that is happening is that many nonprofit groups are getting involved in pushing legislation and ballot propositions. The laws regarding nonprofits are supposed to prevent these organizations from supporting legislation. I can understand their lobbying for funds for research, but I can't understand how they can be allowed to obtain funds to support legislation that is designed to control people.

One thing I have never been able to understand in the push to get rid of tobacco is some of their advertising. I have never understood how they could say that secondhand smoke is more harmful to other people than smoking is to the smoker. To me it does not make any logical sense. A smoker directly inhales the smoke and after that is surrounded by the secondhand smoke. Other people are not around the smoke from that person as much of the time as the smoker himself. This is an example of people using misinformation to push their agenda. Is this not an indication or form of corruption?

Recently, a politician has come out supporting more taxes on cigarettes. While this in itself is not surprising, what really bothers me is that he is supporting putting this tax on cigarettes to fund health care for children. There was an initiative on a recent ballot to raise the tax on cigarettes to fund other children's projects. It appears that the politicians have found that they can get the support of the people for their projects by saying they are doing it for the children. Now the question becomes, are they really doing it for the children? Are they doing it to support other drugs over cigarettes? Or are they doing it to get their hands on more tax money?

The discussion on supporting other drugs is addressed elsewhere in this book. The idea of getting their hands on more tax money, though, deserves a little more discussion here.

A number of years ago, a group of attorney generals of several states got together and sued the tobacco industry and won an extremely large settlement.

This settlement money was supposed to go to tobacco-related projects—things such as tobacco education, health-care costs due to the perceived problems caused by tobacco and such. Over the years since that settlement, there have been many cases in the news of how the majority of this money was being used for everything except what was specified in the settlement. It was being used for roads and bridges. It was also being used for pet projects of politicians. This money was being so misused that many of those attorney generals were quoted as being disgusted with how it was being used. They had fought hard to get it used to help defray the costs they felt the tobacco was costing the states and to help educate the people. They had not fought to have it used for roads, bridges, buildings, and monuments.

For a long time, I kept hearing that Mississippi was the only state that was using its share of the money in accordance with the settlement. The leaders there were saying while Mississippi is one of the poorest states in the union, they were the only ones using the money properly.

With this in mind, how can we believe these politicians who want to get more money from the tobacco industry? How can we believe they will not divert this money to other uses? How can we be sure they will not say that the money collected is more than they expected or needed and decide to put it somewhere else? How can we be sure they are not just doing this because to push their own personal beliefs or agenda? How can we be sure their supporters are not those who realize that by making tobacco more expensive, they can push their legal or illegal drugs? Money corrupts.

I find it interesting that as I am writing this, there is an ad on TV where another politician is pushing for another ballot initiative to fund another project for children to be paid for by another tax on cigarettes. In this area, this appears to be becoming an event that every election is having an initiative for an increase in tobacco tax to support some project for children.

One thing that really bothers me is that politicians are using children to drive their agenda. They say they are going to use this money to benefit the children, and they use children in their ads. If they were really doing it for the children, would they be making their projects dependent on taxes from a product they are trying to get rid of? If they are really trying to get rid of tobacco and do succeed, where is the money they say they are going to raise for the children. If tobacco is eliminated, there will be no tax money and therefore no money for the children. How does this make any sense? How does it make sense to say they are going to help the children by taxing tobacco that they hope will not be there anymore? Are they not just playing a political shell game with our children, and therefore, are they really concerned about our children?

Now let's look at another problem that has arisen. As with the problems with getting rid of alcohol, people start looking for other "narcotics" to help them get through life. (Nature abhors a vacuum.) Since the big push to rid the country of cigarettes, people have started looking to other drugs. In a conversation with my doctor, I mentioned that I thought people were replacing cigarettes with illegal drugs. His response was that they were replacing them with both *legal* and illegal drugs. This indicated to me that doctors were prescribing more drugs to help people cope with their daily lives. This has put more drugs into the medicine cabinets in more homes.

In a recent story on the news, they were discussing the most used prescriptions. They asked if it was heart medicine, blood pressure medicine, cholesterol medicine, or sedatives (narcotics). They said that the sedatives were the most prescribed medicines, which supports my idea that people are always looking for something to make their life easier.

This has also increased the usage of prescription insurance. With this, the cost of insurance is sure to go up.

I looked up in my *Random House College Dictionary* the word "narcotic" and the definition was, "A drug that dulls the senses, induces sleep, and with prolonged usage becomes addictive." If we take a look at many different things in our lives, we would be surprised as to how many of them could be classified as a narcotic.

Food could be classified as a narcotic. Let us take a look at someone after a large Thanksgiving dinner. Their senses are dulled, and they want to sleep. And as for food being addictive, we only need to look at the fact that obesity is now becoming a large problem in this country. This indicates that more and more people are looking for narcotics to get through the daily stress of everyone else telling them what they can and cannot do.

Politics could also be classified as a narcotic. Passing laws to control other people gives the feeling of having solved a problem and dulls the senses to other problems or damage that the laws might cause. The politician becomes lazy and thinks that he only needs to pass laws and spend money to solve problems. Politicians do not want to really look at or analyze the problem. The feeling of power that comes from passing laws and people coming to them to get things done become addictive.

As you can see, what we call drugs are just a subset of narcotics. People throughout time have been seeking out narcotics of all forms. What we need to consider is that if we try to limit the availability of certain narcotics, will we end up moving people to other narcotics? While some of these other narcotics may not be that harmful, a small percentage of each group we move from a narcotic will end up going to those that are more harmful. The more we try to get rid of a narcotic, the larger the group using more dangerous or harmful narcotics will become.

As we have seen, anything that people that find pleasurable, that causes them to relax, and that they enjoy doing frequently could be considered a narcotic. With this in mind and the current mass stampede toward "zero tolerance" of narcotics, what are we going to have left to make our lives enjoyable? If you look around you, you will see that for everything that people find pleasurable, there are people who do not like it. Given the fact that we have become a society that likes to legislate against everything and people are now so predisposed to vote to control other people's lives, all the pleasures of life will eventually be made illegal. All we will have left is sleeping, eating, and working, and those things will have to be done by a set of specific rules.

Maybe we should start looking for the sources of the problems that send people looking for narcotics. We should start looking for the stresses in people's lives that makes them look for narcotics and work on reducing or getting rid of those problems instead of creating more stress by forcing them off of their narcotic of choice.

Another thing I have noticed is that people are becoming more "in your face." This is another indication of the frustrations that are developing because people do not feel they have control of their lives. These are indications of the number and type of people who are likely to look for alternatives to help make their lives easier or more pleasurable.

Listening to the news, I am hearing more government attorneys and police officers discussing the fact that young people are now sneaking their parents' pills in greater numbers than ever before. Why? Well they too, as in the generations before them, are looking for things to help them get through their trials and tribulations. They see their parents using these drugs, so they decide they should try them also. So now instead of sneaking a cigarette out of their mother's purse and going out behind the garage and smoking, they sneak the drugs out of the medicine cabinet. Another advantage to this is that they can take the drugs quickly and not be seen as opposed to being more vulnerable to being seen behind the garage or having the smell of tobacco on them. Also, the effects of many of these drugs are subtler and not as visibly detectable.

Now on to the problem of the more serious drugs. These are frequently found to be available around schools and other places young adults hang around. They are also available to the general public in many places and are not too hard to find.

The drug dealers are usually well tuned to people who are good candidates for their wares. They are also smart businesspeople and know that free samples are a good way to get new people involved in drugs. Early on, these drugs may seem to not be too serious, and people around the users may not even notice that someone is taking them. This is quite different than smoking where people are now more inclined to complain about the smoke or someone smoking.

Once someone starts to get hooked on drugs, several things happen. For one thing, they find they have enjoyed the effect and have a greater desire for the drugs. Another is that the drugs are no longer free, and they rapidly become expensive. Even with the expense, many become very dependent on the drugs and start looking for ways to support their habit. Some will even turn to illegal methods to pay for their addiction. There is a benefit from moving people from cigarettes to drugs. It gives people more things to worry about and the police more crimes to investigate.

Now let's look at the other side of the illegal drug trade. With more people turning to illegal drugs, that means more money is flowing to the drug dealers and suppliers. With more money flowing, the dealers and suppliers are looking for ways to increase their supply. One part of that supply chain is keeping law enforcement from interrupting the supply lines. As we have seen in the war on alcohol, money is a tool that starts being used to corrupt officials to look the other way. Another way to increase the supply is to build larger organizations. The larger organizations now create greater opportunity and more money.

Now that the supply is increased, the need for more outlets is also increased. This may mean moving into other territories controlled by other organizations. This causes friction and possibly fighting among the organizations. In the process, many innocent bystanders may be hurt.

Another way to increase the available clients is to try to move them off of legal and other drugs. One way to do this is to encourage and support efforts to eliminate the less addictive or legal drugs. With large amounts of money flowing, proper laundering and placement of funds can lead to greater demand for these illegal drugs.

This makes me wonder how much of the monies being spent on trying to eliminate tobacco is coming from sales of both legal and illegal drugs. And also, how many well-intentioned organizations are be unknowingly being funded by illegal (and possibly legal) drug money?

I have not heard anyone even mention the impact that all of this is having on the poor in our country. In my estimation, the poor are probably more likely to be smokers. They do not have access to as many things to give them pleasure. Therefore, smoking has been one of the pleasures they had access to.

Now, with the increases in cigarette costs due to large jury awards and the large increases in taxes, that are being legislated and voted in, this group is being taxed disproportionately to their income.

These people are more likely to be seduced by the drug dealers and their free trial offers. If the cost of cigarettes were not increasing so rapidly, they probably would not be as tempted.

Once hooked on these drugs, the dealers will start raising the price. Being hooked, these people will be pushed to find ways to fund their habits. This opens up the possibility of seeking illegal ways of supporting their habit.

This is just another example of how many legislative attempts to control people's lives and choices ends up being paid for by the poor. This helps widen the gap between the classes.

Another interesting fact is that the tobacco companies are legal, taxpaying companies. They generate jobs for people who are just looking to make a living. These people pay taxes and just wish to live a normal, productive life. These are people who are not interested in a criminal life.

So why are we so interested in driving a productive, taxpaying business out of business when we can see it will be replaced by an illegal and non-taxpaying business—a business that is being run by people who do not pay taxes and in many cases turn to other crimes to support their habits? Not only are these illegal businesses not paying taxes, but they are also tax consuming. We have to pay the police to try to eliminate these illegal activities. When the police capture people running these illegal businesses, we then have to use tax money to prosecute them. If these people are then convicted, we have to use our tax money to pay for their incarceration.

Why are we so intent on destroying a legal and tax-generating business and replacing it with ones that are illegal and require us to pay more taxes to control and incarcerate the criminals that run them? Why are we so intent in getting rid of a tax-generating business and replacing it with more dangerous drugs and more dangerous drug dealers?

Yes, tobacco may be a drug that has some unwanted side effects. This is no different than many other things in our daily lives. Many, if not most, drugs that are prescribed by doctors also have various hazardous side effects. The companies that make these drugs are also legal and taxpaying. Their drugs are known to have side effects that even include death. But because this possibility is considered to affect an extremely small number of people compared to the number of people the drug is expected to help, these numbers are glossed over. Why have we become so intent on a negative aspect of smoking that we fail to see the extremely negative aspects of those things that will replace it?

Speaking of legal and taxpaying companies, the manufactures of the over-the-counter cold medicines fit in this category. Again the government has decided that these companies' rights need to be restricted, and the users of these products must be punished for using them. In many areas of the country, the government has required that these products be put behind the pharmacy counter, and those who want to use them must show identification and sign for them. This is not because the FDA has determined that there in a need to control the use of these products. This is because the people have allowed the government to again take more control of what the average citizen is allowed to do. They say it is to control a small percentage of people who use these products to create other drugs. It is interesting that as they are trying to control one thing, they have to put controls on something else. It appears that the only way the government can control something is to put more controls on other things that the average person uses. While to many this may not seem to be too invasive, which straw is it that is going to break the camel's back?

This may not seem to be much of an inconvenience to some, but consider the people who live in the smaller towns where the druggist may only be available from nine to five during the week and in the morning on Saturday. This means that these people can only get these remedies during these times, and if they should start needing them on Saturday afternoon, the government has decided that they don't need them until Monday morning. So what if they have to spend two days with headaches, runny noses, and generally feeling lousy? You must remember that the all-knowing government has determined that this is in your best interest.

Another side benefit of this is that it gives the government another database to use to track what everyone does. The more they know about what people are doing, the better they can design controls on the people.

While I am talking about having to sign for products, I was very surprised and annoyed when I stopped at an office-supply store to buy a can of compressed air to blow the dust out of my computer keyboard. When I walked up to the counter to pay cash, I was surprised that the clerk asked for my driver's license. He had to swipe it in to the register before he could sell me the can of compressed air. I asked him why a senior citizen could not buy a can of compressed air. He said he didn't know, but he was required to take identification from anyone buying the product. I would be interested to find out why a senior citizen is considered such a threat with a can of compressed air that the government needs my personal information. How far are we going to let them go?

So, by taking a very focused view on eliminating tobacco usage and not looking at what other problems we are causing, we are again creating more and larger problems than those we started with. I also fault the media, which was once called the forth estate for not connecting the dots, for not looking any further than what they perceive the public will, and for not reporting on the problems being created.

# Lawyers and Law

For lawyers, the law and the practice of law is like a game of advantage and power. It is a game not unlike football, baseball, or hockey. The object is to get or create an advantage for their client. They do this through courtroom maneuvering to get the best advantage for a client. They also work with politicians to develop laws that help support the politicians' position and please their constituents. They also become politicians themselves where they develop laws to help their position or as a result of pressure from their constituency.

When a lawyer is working for a client, it is his responsibility to give the best possible advice to his client. If he is working on legal documents for a client, it is his duty to create the document to protect the client.

When he is defending a client, his responsibility is to use every legal advantage to get a favorable outcome for the client. This is where they must bring their "A game" to the table and play that game to their fullest abilities.

In these examples, the game is on and the game is to maneuver the rules and laws to achieve the desired outcome. This is what lawyers are supposed to do. But, like a hockey game, when the game is on, they must play to win. The problem I have is that when lawyers are not working for a client, the game does not end.

When lawyers are developing laws, either for a politician or as a politician, the game should not be on. When they are working in this arena, they should not be working for a specific client. At this point, they should be working for all the people. They, in essence, are working for two clients. The game of trying to score for one side or the other no longer applies. They need to balance the desires of the constituency along with their responsibility to uphold the intent set forth by the Founding Fathers.

They should also be looking at history and taking the lessons learned as to the consequences of similar types of legislation. They should not only look at the positive results but also at the negative and the unintended results. Also, if they are working on laws that are designed to control the general public, they really need to look at what freedoms our Founding Fathers gave us and realize that it is those freedoms that have made this country great. To restate a quote I have used elsewhere, Ben Franklin said, "He who sacrifices freedom for security deserves neither."

Also, when considering laws that restrict the rights of the average citizen, lawyers should make sure, like the Constitution says, the laws apply to everyone. Our Founding Fathers put this in to prevent the development of an elitist group with special powers within this county. This speaks to the duty of using responsibility when exercising the right to make laws.

Recently I have been the victim of a bankruptcy proceeding. I had bought into some investments that were to be managed by a company. I was careful to spread my risk over several investments. Also, these investments were in my name and it was not the company that I had invested in. They were just to manage the investments.

This company mismanaged their money and some money others had invested in the company. This resulted in the company filing for bankruptcy.

At this point, lawyers became involved along with the bankruptcy court. Through all of this, lawyers were racking up many billable hours working on every legal action they could find.

While they were spending all of this time on the bankruptcy, they did not appear to spend any time on the legal requirements of the company to manage my (and many others) investments. They basically ignored the legal commitments of the company in regard to the investments they were to manage or the individuals who had investments that the company was to manage.

These lawyers ran up many millions of dollars in fees. As the company did not have that kind of money, they convinced the bankruptcy court that even though many of the investors had investments that they owned and that the company was only to manage, this was now part of the assets of the company. Because of this, they wanted to use some of this money to pay their fees. Not only this, the losses in fees that the company would have received had they continued properly managing the investments were to be made up from those who had legal rights to the investments instead of from the fees from the investments themselves.

Also, the rights that were in the investors' contracts were no longer enforced and they could change them so they could further take money from the investors.

All of this was so that the lawyers and those they put in place to run what was left of the company could take big fees and commissions from those who legally owned the investments.

Another aspect of this is that these investments became so mis-managed that they did harm to those we invested in. Many of those we had invested in had been so damaged that they are about to turn around and sue those of us who made the investments for breach of contract and financial harm, which will lead to more lawyers' fees.

It is not just us investors who feel this is wrong and has been bungled. Other companies that are in the same business have indicated that what has been done with this bankruptcy is bordering on criminal. They have indicated that they would be willing to supply expert witness to that fact.

# Insurance Companies

When you buy insurance, you think you are being insured against unexpected loss or injury. When you insure your home, you think you will have it repaired or replaced when it is damaged or destroyed by something that was not under your control. When you buy medical insurance, you expect that your medical bills will be covered if you become sick or injured. The same goes for auto, life, and other types of insurance.

Well this may be how it used to be, but now that the lawyers and courts have gotten involved, this is not the way it is anymore. Insurance policies used to be one or a few pages, and now they come with a book of all the exceptions that are not covered. There are so many exceptions that unless you continually study the ever-changing book, you really have no idea as to what coverage you actually have. Even if you do study the book, the insurance companies and their lawyers can probably find some way to interpret the book that will say that you are not covered.

It makes me wonder if the amount of money the insurance companies spend on defining and finding ways around their rules could not be put to better use. If all of this money were put into the pool to pay for damages, how many less exceptions would be necessary?

Also, these insurance companies are very active in political causes. They spend or give a large amount of their money supporting politicians. They also spend lots of money lobbying government officials at all levels to get favorable laws to allow them to have exceptions in their policies. They also use a lot of money to support passages of laws controlling the actions of the people. They seem to think it is appropriate to have the government tell people what to do when it is to their benefit.

It seems they are more interested in controlling people's lives than they are in insuring things that may happen.

What about insurance and global warming. What does insurance have to do with global warming? Well, when I travel, I usually have my small dog with me. From time to time on the road, I must stop and go into stores. Being away from home, I cannot leave my dog at home while I go shopping. Even though the outside temperature may be in the seventies or low eighties, the sun beating down on the car will raise the inside temperature quite rapidly. Because of this, I will go out of my way to find shade for the car.

On a recent trip, I started noticing that it was impossible to find shade in many large parking lots. While many of them did have some trees and shrubs, I did not see any trees or shrubs over ten to fifteen feet tall and none of them were giving very much shade. I started thinking back to my younger days, and I remembered that most of the businesses had large trees around their buildings and parking areas to give shade and make it more pleasant for their customers.

Why would these businesses not want to make the shopping experience more pleasurable for their customers? I am sure they would want to make the experience more pleasurable to encourage more shopping, so there must be some other reason.

One of the possible reasons is the cost of land and putting in large trees would take up some room that could be used for parking. But this does not make much sense, as most of the time I find there is a large excess of available parking, especially in the hotter months. People do not want to shop as much in the hotter times because of the hot cars.

Another possibility I came up with is that large trees have a cost to maintain and the bean counters at the larger stores and shopping centers look at this number as an expense and not as an encouragement to have people shop at their stores.

The final possibility is the fact that these large trees have an insurance risk. Branches or other factors may pose a risk to cars parked under or near these trees. This means the bean counters at the insurance companies are now involved. They have a tendency to consider all risk as unacceptable. With this in mind, they will want to increase the risk premiums on stores that have large trees and they will also press to have these types of trees removed from any property that they insure. This is probably one of the major reasons you will only see small trees and shrubs in parking lots.

What does this have to do with global warming? Many large cities are discovering that their average summer temperatures are rising. One of the major causes they are finding is the fact that more and more of their cities are being covered with blacktop and this is absorbing and retaining heat in the summertime. They are finding also that the fact that there is less and less shading of this blacktop is also increasing the heat absorption and heating of the city.

So while the cities are struggling with trying to reduce the summer heating of their cities, the insurance companies are working to get rid of the large trees and the shade they give. So yes, insurance companies should be held liable in the discussions of global warming.

I have been wondering if the insurance companies are not more interested in spending money on trying to reduce their costs than it would cost to properly pay their claims.

I will admit that I think the legal system with its excessive awards for claims such as a million dollars for someone who spilled hot coffee on himself are having an adverse effect on settling claims. I also wonder if the fact that insurance is becoming more and more reticent to pay claims is not also causing this.

It would be interesting to know how much money these insurance companies are spending on "risk management" lawyers to write their books of exceptions and lawyers to fight the claims of their customers.

Insurance is supposed to be there to help protect the customer from actual losses due to some random event. It is not supposed to be there to inflict more damage and injury due to the fighting over the whether the claim is legitimate or covered by the policy.

I wonder what would happen if the insurance companies reduced the amount they spent on trying to find more and more exceptions to their policies and if they would stop paying their bureaucrats and lawyers so much to fight legitimate claims. I also wonder what would happen if they stopped spending so much on political lobbying to get favorable laws to allow them to avoid paying legitimate claims. I wonder if this would not allow these companies to more amicably pay their claims and also improve their perception among their customers and the general public.

Another thing that must be done to achieve this reduction in costs and this adversarial situation between insurance companies, their customers, and those making claims is a change in the court system. We need to find some way to limit court claims to those of actual loss. The costs and losses caused by someone spilling a hot cup of coffee (we all know that coffee is hot and should be handled carefully) is far less than the million dollars that was awarded. There are many other cases where the awards far exceeded the actual loss or damage that was actually incurred. The lawyers for these cases frequently say that someone needs to be punished for the incident.

The fact is that in most cases the only ones who are actually punished is the general public, which ends up paying for the settlement. This is both in the fact that everyone's premiums for insurance go up and the fact that the insurance companies are spending more and more to find ways to limit what they will cover and are liable for.

Both sides of this problem need to sit down and quit being so focused on how they can get an advantage and start looking for ways they can get the system back to what it is supposed to do—protect people from losses from some random event.

# For the Greater Good

"For the greater good," "for the common good," and "for the good of the people" are all phrases that are becoming more prevalent in our society today. These phrases are all very similar in meaning. They only differ in the words they use and the word order. These phrases also have the power to place the focus on the perceived good and in so doing, they tend to limit any focus on whether these perceived goods have any negative aspects.

I see more and more police and fire departments using "for the greater good" as their motto. When I was growing up, the motto of these organizations was, "To protect and serve." I am seeing advertisements for products on TV that say they are directed toward people and organizations that are working for "the greater good."

Let's take a look of the structure of these phrases. The first word is "for." When I look up synonyms for "for," some of the choices are "to go to," "toward," "in favor of," and "in order to." This indicates that someone or some group is going to unilaterally do something they want or have decided is needed. Such as *in order to* do what they think is right.

Secondly, let's look at "the greater." When I look up synonyms for "greater," I get words like "excellent," "bigger," "finer," and "larger." This indicates a higher power or something that more excellent and is above the average mortal. There is no indication as to who or what this higher power is or what this higher power stands for or desires.

Finally, let's look at the word "good." When I look up synonyms for "good," I get words like "moral," "upright," "virtuous," and "worthy." This has the connotation of being better or the best thing to happen. This does not define what good is nor does it have any indication as to whose good we are talking about. Is it your good, my good, or someone else's good?

Another thing this indicates is that in the user's opinion, things are not now great or good, and they have the answers to correct the situation. But it does not indicate they are concerned about what other people think about their idea.

Let's now look at the phrase, "To protect and serve." The first word is "to." When I look up synonyms for "to," I get words like "until," "toward," "as far as," and "up to." This indicates movement toward doing something.

The second word is "protect." The synonyms I found for "protect" are "guard," "preserve," "cover," "insulate," "defend," "safeguard," and "save." This indicates that there is some respect for those things they are working with. This does not indicate that they are trying to make judgment or change anything but that they have a desire to keep the things from being altered or destroyed.

The final word is "serve." Again, when I look up the synonyms for "serve," I find words like "enlist," "help," "follow," "promote," and "attend." These words indicate help or attention to my problem or situation. This does not seem to in any way indicate a desire to change my way of thinking or doing.

Does this mean that those police and fire departments that have changed to "For the greater good" have also changed their focus from helping and protecting to a position of judgment and pushing change to their beliefs? If this is the case, are we to expect that for each police or fire jurisdiction we are going to be subject to the desires and whims of that jurisdiction? Are they setting themselves up as an equal to the legislative bodies that govern that jurisdiction? And as an extension of this, do they feel they should be able to establish their own rules (laws) that apply to their jurisdictions without the need or consideration of the voters in that jurisdiction or the requirements of the Constitution?

I am sure that it not only police and fire departments that are using these phrases. They are becoming more pervasive all the time.

Let's look at some of the historical usages of the phrase "For the greater good" and its variations.

I am sure you can probably find many usages of these phrases in the works and ideas of people like Stalin and Lenin. They were able to convince many people they had a better way of government and social structure. They would have to convince people that a government that defined what and how people were to do or act was for the greater good. They had to convince people that the government deciding what was good and bad was in their best interest. They had to convince people that the government always knew best about everything. They had to convince people that their individual rights, liberties, and desires would be best served by those who knew better—the government. To do this, they would have to convince people that it was for "the greater good" that they should cede their abilities, desires, and hopes to the government. Of course Stalin and Lenin were going to be the ones that established the government the way they thought it should be.

Hitler probably used similar phrases to help take control of Germany. He was known to use and/or create disasters as a basis for new laws giving the government and himself more power. I feel sure he used phrases like "for the good of the people" to convince many that these new laws are needed. After having problems with conflicting laws, he probably used phrases like "for the good of the people" or "for the greater good" to convince the delegates at Nuremberg to develop laws that essentially said that if "we" or "the government" don't like something, it is against the law.

There are probably many people who take these phrases at face value and feel that those things put forth "for the greater good" are always good for everyone.

I think it was P. T. Barnum who stated, "You can fool some of the people all the time, all the people some of the time but you can't fool all the people all the time." This applies in this case. Those who continually focus on the word "good" will probably be fooled into believing everything that is being put forth is good. Those who are not so focused on the word "good" and who are willing to look at all aspects of what is being proposed will not be so fooled into believing in everything that is proposed in this manner.

# Socialism

Socialism is a very seductive concept. My *Random House College Dictionary* defines "socialism" as "a theory or system of social organization that advocates the ownership and control of industry, capital, land, etc., by the community as a whole." Many people need and are comforted by structure. The socialistically defined structure is not the only definition of structure.

One of the first problems with socialistic structure is that there are almost as many different socialistic structures as there are people who want socialism. All of these people have their own ideas of how the different elements of the structure should put in place.

Another problem is that the structure put in place must be a one-size-fits-all, and everyone must live by the end result. This leads to power struggles between the various ideas and ways of implementing socialism. This is an ongoing problem and tends to lead to corruption in order to get an advantage.

This reminds me of a story I heard. If you take a bunch of crabs and put them in a bucket, some of them will start to crawl out. As the other crabs see them trying to escape, they will pull them back into the bucket.

Socialism is so structured that, by its very design, it tends to limit and suppress creativity. Unless something is built into the structure, it will not be allowed. This tends to frustrate creative people to the point that they give up and withdraw.

Also, this means that because of your social status at birth, you may be limited as to what education you are allowed to have. This will mean that many children who could grow up and make great contributions to society would be stopped by that society before they even have a chance to show what they could do.

In a true socialistic society, everything is done by rules and laws. For example, waiters' and waitresses' salary and tips are defined by the socialistic structure. Frequently this may also include the fact that cannot be terminated from their position. This means that these people have no incentive to do a better job. Eventually, many of these people develop the attitude that they do not have care about the service they give their customers. They can take their own sweet time to serve the customer. They do not have to worry about getting the food to the table in a timely fashion so that it is not delivered cold.

I remember hearing stories about when the Berlin Wall fell. Among them were stories about how the waiters and waitresses, on the East German side of the wall, were somewhat in shock at the demands of the people from West Germany. They really had never learned how to give service because under the old system, it didn't matter. They had a hard time adjusting to a world where their compensation was dependent on the service they gave as opposed to just being based on being there.

As I am writing this, I am remembering something I saw on a TV show recently. I have seen similar stories on different shows, but this was recent enough for me to remember more of the details. This is a very good example of a micro-socialistic society with its up and downsides.

A wife had for some reason contacted the show saying there seemed to be some problems with the family's home life, and she was looking for help. The show sent cameras out to the home to see how they were living.

The wife was happy to share all the rules (socialistic structure) she had set up for the family so the household would run the way she wanted it to.

One thing was the organization of the closets. Shirts were to be put at one end of the closets in order of type and color. This was to be followed by skirts for the girl. These skirts were also to be placed from left to right, in order, by another specific set of rules. This was then to be followed by dresses, again governed by their own specific set of rules. The same type of structure applied to the dressers and their contents.

If the wife (mother) went into the children's room and found anything out of order in the closet, she would remove everything from the closet, throw them on the bed, and make the child put it all back in the proper order.

The wife also took care of all the money and bills. Her rules required that her husband did not have any cash in his wallet and if he wanted to use the debit card, he had to notify her first and get her permission.

There was a large couch in their living room, and no one was allowed to lounge on it because it would mess up the pillows and that was against her rules.

Every week the family would all make suggestions for something they would like to do for entertainment. According to the wife's rules, she was the one who would make the final decision as to what the family would do.

I am sure she probably felt that she was doing this "for the greater good" of the family.

The family was on the show. The father, son, and daughter were sitting there quietly. None of them looked very happy. The TV show had a family relations' expert come in and talk to the family. After some discussion, the expert commented that if this structure continued, it would probably not be too long before the husband would have enough and leave, even though the couple said they loved each other very much.

The family did consent to having some ongoing and in-depth counseling to see if the situation could be mitigated.

This example contains all the elements of a socialistic structure—one person (or small group) is making the rules about what everyone must do in all aspects of their lives. This person is also the one who determines whether the rules are being followed and who determines the punishment.

This example also shows many of the downsides to this type of structure. People feel unappreciated and that their needs and ideas are being ignored out of hand. The strain of this was showing in the withdrawal of the rest of the family and the direction toward the eventual breakup of the family.

This structure may be good for the one who developed it, and it may make her very comfortable. This is a good example of focusing on those aspects the creator liked and how the failure to look around at what the structure is causing could end up with the breakdown of the family.

If this socialist type of structure were put into effect on a much larger group of people, it might be harder to see the problems caused. These would be much more varied and it would be harder to tie the problems back to the source. But the final result would be a breakdown of many parts of the structure, resulting in its collapse.

There are many examples of this happening in the countries that formed the Soviet Union and the Eastern Block.

One large problem that occurred in these countries where the government had a heavy hand in controlling the people is that a large percentage of the population turned to alcohol and other drugs. The more oppressive and corrupt the governments became, the greater the problem of the people using alcohol, drugs, and anything else they could find to help them cope with it.

# Performing Arts and Socialism

During political campaigns, it seems that members of the performing arts become a very visible force. Many of them are out supporting candidates whose main agenda is more governmental social programs.

Understanding where these people are coming from is the first step in understanding their motives. Let us take actors as an example. These people look for scripts to perform. These scripts are usually a clear and concise description of a series of events that has a beginning and end. This completeness gives the performer a sense of security in the task he is about to take on. This script also includes things such as emotion, action, and suspense. Once the script is written and finalized, there are very few, if any, unexpected events that will occur. In other words, it is a complete and self-contained microcosm.

Why is socialism so attractive to performing artists? Well, pure socialism is a set of laws and rules describing how all people are to act and how they are to live their lives. This is not much different than what they would look for in a script for a play or movie. They are looking for something they are interested in and a sense of security in knowing what they will be doing in the future.

Again, this is looking at things through glasses with a pair of toilet paper cores taped on them.

One thing about scripts is that they are very concise about what is to happen, but it has been found that many successful movies include many scenes that were not scripted. This improvisation is done before any changes are made to the script. These scenes were allowed by the director and later included in the final product.

Socialism is also concise about things that are to happen and in that it gives a sense of security about what will happen in the future. Once written into law, socialism becomes a very stiff frame that does not allow non-scripted actions. This means that everyone must stick strictly to the script and any improvisation is not allowed because the script is now set in law. There is no director who can allow improvisation before the script or law is changed.

Actors and producers are usually presented with many different scripts that cover many different views on life and how it should be portrayed. These actors and producers have the opportunity to pick and choose which script they like or portray a version of what they think is correct. With socialism, there is only one script that everyone must follow without improvisation.

There are photographers who have been very successful in photographing in only black and white. As well, there are musicians who are successful in writing music that uses only one or two octaves. There are painters who create beautiful pictures using a very narrow palette of colors.

If we take these ideas and put them into a socialistic form, we can say that all photographers must photograph in black and white and use the example of the successful black-and-white pictures. All musicians must write in only the one or two octaves. Also, all painters must stay in the narrow palette of colors that produced the masterpieces that painted in that fashion.

I believe it can be seen that people like to live in their comfort zone and if they feel successful in their comfort zone, they want others to live in that comfort zone also. This is somewhat understandable, but it does not allow for the improvisation that makes life more interesting.

Another thing that I find interesting is that social programs tend to be turned into laws. These laws are then administered by low-level bureaucrats. These bureaucrats in effect control or censor the recipients' actions. The recipient must do things exactly the way they are told or lose their benefits. This is interesting coming from members of a group that has fought for years against censorship on their industry.

# Religion and Socialism

This, to many, may seem a strange combination. Why would I so link religion and socialism? I do this because of man's influence on religion. *Man's influence on religion?* It is supposed to be religion's influence on man!

Yes, religion has had a large influence on man, but it is man who has taken the basic fundamentals of religion and used them to further his ideas.

An example of this might be found in a couple of ideas put forth in the Bible. The Bible talks about leaving behind your worldly possessions and following the Lord God so that you will forever dwell in heaven. When I look at many of the religious groups and leaders, it seems that they are becoming more interested in getting their hands on your worldly possessions. It seems like they are saying, "Give us your worldly possessions and follow us, and God will take you into heaven."

On the news, they were recently comparing some movie star and a religious leader. They were saying that both of them believed that anyone who did not believe in their exact form of religion would not go to heaven. From what I understand of the Bible, it is the Lord who said he who follows my teachings shall dwell in heaven. I do not remember anywhere in the Bible where it says that you must belong to one specific religion or another. This even leaves door open to the possibility that anyone, Christian or any other person, who lives his life in a good and loving manner shall dwell in heaven. It does not imply that anyone who does not have the Bible as his or her guide is an infidel.

Let's start with the Ten Commandments. Lest you think that by talking about the Ten Commandments I am trying to focus on a particular religion, many years ago I heard a religious scholar state, "The Ten Commandments in some form are found in almost all of the major religions."

Basically, these commandments talk about how people should interact. They say people should not "covet" what other people have and respect other people's rights.

As an aside, doesn't this sound a little bit like what our Founding Fathers tried to put forth in the Constitution?

Having said this about the commandments, it interesting that they do not talk about what the punishment should be for each of these guidelines. Instead, the judgment and punishment was to be left to a power that was above man and not to man's discretion.

Another thing that is prevalent in religions is that they are the teachings of a higher power. The writers do not talk about them as laws but as those things people should do to create harmony between the people. The writers did not talk of them as laws but as things that should be taught.

Back in earlier times, governments were not involved in teaching and it fell mostly to the religious groups to do the teaching. Many early discoveries were made by monks and the like.

The commandments are also very important because they directly address many human foibles. They address those qualities or traits in people that tend to make individuals feel superior to others, those traits that make people think that because something exists it should belong to them, and those traits of people that make them think they and they alone have all the right answers. They are based on the realization that all people have something to contribute and no one should deprive another of his or her contribution.

As I have said, these ideas are to be taught. They are not a definition of a political structure to be put in place. They did not specify that man was to use these as a way to gain power. Power is something that is "coveted." They are a good example of the idea that we should educate and not legislate or impose our ideas.

With this in mind, we look at what has happened to religion from early times to now. The main thing that has happened is that religions require man to pass along the teaching. Now that we have man involved with all his foibles, we start to see him interjecting his thoughts and ideas along with the original teachings.

As time goes along and these ideas are passed along, man starts building on not only the original ideas, but also the ideas of his predecessors. As this progresses, those interjections of man start to overtake the original teachings.

I keep hearing that many religions are losing their following. I wonder if this is not directly related to the fact that many of these institutions are straying further and further from their basic ideas of teaching. They have moved from teaching the fundamentals of respect and the benefits of that to a position of teaching that their parishioners need to go out and pass laws and tell other people how they must live their lives. They have stopped teaching people how to better live their own lives and are now teaching that it is in people's best interest to go out and control other people's lives.

Many of today's religions came from groups that split off from other religions. Why did these splits occur? Is it because man caused the original religious group to become corrupt and the splinter group wanted to get back to the basic teaching? Or is it because the leaders of the splinter groups wanted to have the power over the group and had to split off in order to get that power?

I think we can see this activity even today. There are many religious groups or factions that just want to teach these basics and live in peace with everyone else. There are some religious factions who want to control all aspects of the lives of their group and seek isolation from the "infidels" around them. There are groups who want to teach the rules as modified by man and feel these should be imposed on others. There are groups still within some of the major religions who feel so strongly that the ideas put forth by their leaders are the only rules that they are willing to fight and have armed confrontations with other factions within their religion.

When it comes right down to it, many of our churches or religious leaders are not much different than politicians. They need to convince people to follow them. They need to raise money to further their causes and to build large and fancy buildings to use to put forth their ideas. The more people they convince to follow them, the more money they can collect to make their life easier, feed their ego, and push their ideas. This, as with politics, becomes a vicious circle. The more success they have, the more they want and the more they will drive their ideas hoping to get more people convinced that they have the answers to all their problems.

What has all of this got to do with socialism? It is those religions that have been so influenced by man that they think it is their religious duty to impose their version of what is right on everyone else. This is not only being done by the center of the religious groups. In many cases it is being driven by local religious groups.

The reason there are so many different religious groups is that they all have differing opinions on what they think is right and what the rules are and how they should be applied. With this in mind, how can we let any particular religious group get control and have their ideas put into laws?

In fact, I thought the Constitution called for separation of church and state. If this is the case, how can we allow religions to tell their followers to push their ideas for the creation of laws? If they can do this, then the government should be able to tell them what they should teach and believe.

Here is an example of how the line defining the separation of church and state is becoming more and more blurred. A friend of mine told me of an elderly relative couple who had lived in their house for years. The church next door wanted to expand their parking lot, so they went to the local government and convinced them to use their power of eminent domain to force the people to sell their family home. I am sure the politicians involved in this were looking for more influence and felt it was worth ignoring the Constitution.

Luke 6:31 in the Bible states, "Do to others as you would have them do to you." If this is to be taken literally, if the churches wish to impose their ideas and will on the government, the government should have the right to impose its will on the churches. Do these religious groups and organizations really want the government telling them what they can or can't do? A similar statement probably appears in many of the other religions and the same rules should apply. For those who are not into religion, this phrase can also be found translated into common usage in the English language. The phrase is "What goes around comes around."

Religious leaders are also getting into trying to tell us what can be taught in schools. They are trying to say that the scientific view of evolution should be replaced with the biblical view of creationism. This appears to have a couple of problems. One is that if the religious leaders do not feel that their stand and what they are teaching their people is strong enough that they must tell everyone else what they must do. Another problem is that this is another case where the constitutional declaration of the government shall make no law regarding religion should be considered. Also, these actions are the type that lead to the old activity of burning books because they do not say what you want to hear.

We must remember that by limiting the scopes of information people are exposed to, we are also limiting the amount of growth a person can have.

I find it very interesting that religions have been able to get the ACLU to take their desires and ideas to the courts to get their way. They have worked to get one religious group's public displays removed because some other religious group thought they were offensive to their ideas.

If this group is supposedly so interested in the constitutional rights of people, why then are they not going to court against the religious groups? If we are to have true separation of church and state, is it also not as important to have religious groups not try to get their agenda put into law? Should they not be going after the religious groups that are preaching to their flock and telling them how and what they should vote for?

Does not the entry of religious groups into the world of politics move them out of the realm of protection of religious freedoms? Does this not make them a political entity? Should they still have all the religious protections of the Constitution and be considered as any other religious group? They should be either considered a religious group or a political group. They should not be able to hide behind their religion.

One good example is when these religious groups hold large gatherings and invite politicians to speak. They then will give the support of their religion to a particular candidate. They are using their powers as leaders of a religion to tell their people that they should vote as the group sees fit and not as the individuals they are supposed to be under the Constitution.

One group of laws that were enacted in many states are called the "blue laws." These are laws that were pressed by religious groups such as the rules against selling liquor on Sunday mornings because people should not be drinking, they should be in church. For some religions, Sunday morning is not their time of worship. These laws are then favoring one religion over another. Is this not another case of the government favoring one religion over another?

Personally, I do not feel easy about the fact that the Constitution gives me the right to practice my religious beliefs as I see fit, but at the same time, we have religious leaders trying to have the government to impose their religious ideas on people. Is this what the Founding Fathers wanted when they established the separation of church and state?

# Police and Privilege

When I was growing up, I was taught that police and other governmental enforcement agencies were to be taken from citizens of the United States. The founding fathers felt they should be no different than the average citizen except that their job was to enforce the laws, much like the milkman's job was to deliver the milk.

This idea can be seen in the stories of earlier times. In small towns all over the country, the owner of the mercantile or the blacksmith held the job of the sheriff. If the sheriff needed deputies, he would swear in other townspeople to help out. These were the average people of town.

Another indication that average people were to enforce the law is the fact that we, as average people, have the right to make citizen arrests.

This indicates that the people have no more rights than the police, and the police are to have no more rights than the people. When either citizens or police officers make arrests, they have the backing of the laws and are considered to be enforcing the laws of the country.

We must consider that police, as a group, are not different than the average population of the country. They have the same foibles as the rest of the population. This means that they, as a group, will have their share of good and bad people. Just because they put on a uniform and badge does not magically make them perfect. It just means that their full-time job is to enforce the laws while the freeing the rest of us to do our jobs.

We pay police officers to spend the time necessary to investigate crimes, search for criminals, and so on. For us to do this would take us away from our jobs. Our businesses might suffer or fail or our bosses might get tired of us being gone and fire us.

Now that we have given these responsibilities to the police, it does not mean we have given them any more rights than we have. We have not given them to right to race their police car down city streets at ninety miles per hour in the middle of the night without warning lights or siren. This action resulting in an accident and death.

We didn't give them the right to take their motorcycle up a closed off ramp and slam it into a pile of construction material, resulting in the officer's death.

We did not give them the right, while on duty, to stop women drivers in order to meet them or get their addresses. We did not give them the right to use their "authority" to blackmail some of these women into having sex with them.

We did not give them the privilege to race down the road or to run stop signs because they are late for their dinner.

When they are off duty and break the laws, we did not give them the right to have their buddies cover it up.

The government is requiring us to do more and more law enforcement. We are to determine if someone is old enough to do something. Business owners are required to determine if someone is has reached the arbitrarily and politically established age limit to do or buy something.

A business owner is required to have my driver's license scanned to buy a can of compressed air so that I could blow the dust out of my computer keyboard. Business owners are required to check IDs before selling cigarettes or alcohol.

I remember gentler times when parents could send their kids down to the store to pick up some cigarettes or beer just to get them out of the house and doing something. This upset no one and the merchants usually knew these people and did not question it.

Also, people are now more often required to enforce federal laws regarding immigration. We are to check the papers of anyone we hire to see if they are here legally, and we must also be able to determine if the papers they have are legal or forgeries. These people should have been checked at the border. That is what the border patrol and immigration services were created to do.

Now that we have more and more "political laws and crimes" and a large number of them are more and more intrusive into people's private lives, the police are not capable to properly enforce these laws. The politicians have decided that the people must be more involved in the day-to-day enforcement of their laws. This means that individuals are required to do more of the job we hired the police to do. Given this and the fact that most police are required to carry their guns even when they are off duty, the people should also be required to carry guns.

If the people are to do the job of the police, they should also have the same requirements and perks as the police. They should also be allowed to speed down the roads without lights or sirens. They should not have to worry about coming to a complete stop at a stop sign or stoplight.

# Educate or Legislate

We as a country have moved from the idea that education is important to the idea that legislation is important.

We are seeing this in our religious groups. They have stopped teaching respect for other people's rights and ideas and have gone to "legislating" within their sphere of influence that everyone should act and believe the way they want them to.

We are seeing this in our schools where we are narrowing the scope of the schools to teach only the 3 "R's", "Reading, wRighting and aRithmetic" without teaching the social skills and the arts. Much of this change is coming from religious groups who take exception to different aspects of the curriculum and politicians who need the money to foster their own agendas.

The lack of social skill education in the schools is showing itself in these schools as fighting, degradation, and even shootings. On a recent episode of *The Oprah Winfrey Show*, they presented a program used in several schools. They took all the students from a class (i.e., junior or senior) and put them together in an auditorium. They asked them questions such as who had been made fun of. They had those students move to the other side of the auditorium. They then discussed with them how it made them feel. They then asked for those who were making fun of other students to do the same. They did this with many different social problems and created a dialogue about these problems. After a day of doing this, many of the social problems between these students disappeared, and the staff spent less time dealing with social problems.

This was a good example of how trying to legislate social problems had not worked, but when people were educated on social interactions, the problems were greatly reduced. While education may not completely solve social problems, it is a good example of how education can go a long way to reducing the social problems to a manageable level.

A good example of how education works where legislation does not is that of our pets. We can make all the rules and laws we want, but the only way to get our pets to obey them is to educate them. We have to teach them the social skills we want them to have. Just yelling at them that they are not doing the right thing does not work.

Something that I have been thinking about is that maybe we should start teaching manners and respect in the early years such as kindergarten and the first few grades. I think that we should be teaching some of the basic skills such as how to set a table. This could include casual table setting up to formal table setting. Another thing is how to a gentleman seats a lady at a formal table and the proper way to sit and eat at a formal table.

Another thing that has been shown to create respect between sexes and races is formal or ballroom-type dancing. This teaches children how to respectfully have contact with other people. It teaches them to respect the other person's space. Also, it teaches the proper way to ask someone else how to dance also helps teach how to respectfully approach another person and how to respectfully respond to someone's approach.

I am sure many of you have some other good ideas on how to accomplish some of the same results, and I am not trying to say I have the only answer. The main thing I am trying to say is that I think that if we do a little more focus on proper interaction and respect in the earlier years, children will have fewer problems and be better prepared to accept their education in the later years. I feel that teachers in these later years will have to spend less time on discipline and have more time to actually educate children.

One thing that I think people are doing with education that is having a negative effect is that they are becoming too focused on the smaller number of problem children and forgetting to educate the majority of good children.

As another example, years ago when I was learning to drive, we did not have as many or as restrictive traffic laws. I was taught many of the social skills of driving as well as the technical skills needed.

Speed limits were not as restrictive, and on the open roads, there were many places that did not have a speed limit. I was taught that road and driving conditions were the important restrictions on speed. If you were on the open road, the weather conditions, the road conditions, and the amount and speed of the traffic were the things to consider. If the weather was bad, you went slower than you might be able to go a good-weather day. If the traffic was moving at a relative speed, you did not drive slower or faster than the rest of the traffic. You did not obstruct traffic nor did you try to run over the other drivers.

When there were multiple lanes of traffic in your direction, you stayed to the right so that if someone felt like going faster than you thought was right, they could safely pass you on the left. I have talked to people who stay to the left on multi-lane roads. Their answer to why they do this is that they pay taxes for the roads and have the right to use whichever lane they want. If this is taken further and they do not have to follow the laws and courtesies, does it mean that because they pay taxes for the roads and can use whichever lane they choose, they can also use the lanes on the other side of the median? After all, they have paid for the right to use the road according to their own ideas of the laws and courtesies.

When I was learning to drive, when you were going to pass a car, you let them know you were going to pass, and then you sped up if necessary and passed them. You did not just get up beside them and stay there for extended periods of time. Also, if you were being passed, especially on a two-lane road, you yielded to the vehicle passing you. This could even mean slowing down as you were being passed, if it would make it safer for the vehicle passing you.

You were taught to give extra consideration to larger and less maneuverable vehicles such as trucks. If you were to pass them, you were to do it as expediently as possible and not cut in too soon or slow down and obstruct them after passing.

When traveling on a road that did not allow passing, if the road in front of you was clear and there were four or five or more vehicles behind you, you pulled off and let them pass.

When traveling in mountains, the downhill traffic had the right of way, as they could not stop as easily as you.

Also, anytime you were driving, you were to be aware of your surroundings and think about where you might go if a problem arose. You should also be aware of parked cars, as at any time one of those parked cars could suddenly pull in front of you.

In other words, we were taught we did not own the road. We were taught we had to share it with others, and they had as much right to the road as we did. We were also taught to be sure that everyone's rights were respected and that we should use the common courtesies of the road.

We have now come to a time where people do not depend on courtesy but laws, which in many cases make it impossible to be courteous. We now have speed limits that change every few blocks and speed limits that are overly restrictive for road conditions or very radically different for similar roads and road condition. We have electronic enforcement of these crazy laws that try to reduce our driving to the mechanical precision of a Swiss watch.

We now have people who think they own the road and do not feel they have to yield to any other drivers. We have people who are driving considerably less than the speed limit, and when being passed, they speed up and stay beside the car attempting to pass, even to the extent of being well over the speed limit. They may even stay beside them if the passing car tries to slow down and let them go on.

There is another thing those who think that because they pay taxes they have a right to the road (and can use whatever lane they want or go slow if they want) need to consider. They need to consider that large trucks pay a lot more road taxes than they do and they tend to realize they do not own the road but must share it with all the other drivers. They have spent enough time on the road that they have learned that by practicing the common courtesies of the road, their lives and the lives of others around them are much easier and safer.

We have people sitting side-by-side at a stoplight, and when the light turns green, they stay side-by-side for miles after the light even though they are doing ten to fifteen miles per hour less than the speed limit and have a number of cars behind them.

We have police officers who drive in the left lane on multi-lane roads even if there are no cars in the right lane. We also have police officers who feel they have the right to substantially exceed the posted speed limit even though they show no indication of any emergency situation.

I have even had the experience of flagging down a police officer to report a problem in my neighborhood. This officer had just run a stop sign and was upset I had flagged him down. He told me to hurry up and tell him my problem because he was late for dinner.

One thing I find quite amazing is the number of police officers hurt or killed on the job. I do not mean those shot by some bank robber trying to get away or in some other confrontation with a criminal. What I am talking about are officers who are injured, killed, or who harm someone else because they failed to follow the same rules that they themselves are charged with enforcing.

Some examples are after the Northridge Earthquake in California, when the freeways were heavily damaged. A highway patrol officer was trying to stop traffic from traveling onto a collapsed section of the freeway. He tried to flag down a vehicle racing toward him. This vehicle happened to be another highway patrol vehicle. The officer in that vehicle just waved back at the other officer and continued speeding right off of a collapsed bridge and killed himself.

Another incident was a motorcycle officer who had just finished his night shift and was racing home. There was an off ramp that was closed for construction and he took it anyway. During the prior day, the construction crew had moved a large amount of construction material onto the roadway. This motorcycle officer failed to see this in time and crashed into it, killing himself.

Another officer racing to an incident in the middle of the night did not slow for red lights at intersections and was involved in a fatal accident.

These and other officers like them were given hero funerals for killing themselves breaking the laws they were supposed to enforce.

On a recent trip, I stopped at a motel and found a good example of drivers and social skills. This motel had several large parking areas. The closer in parking areas were suitable for cars with a limited amount of space for getting your car in or out. Other areas were capable of holding larger vehicles all the way up to semi-trailer trucks. The closer car parking was almost full when a driver driving a large U-Haul truck drove through the almost empty larger parking area and maneuvered the truck in to the smaller parking area and parked in a space for a car. This vehicle was much longer than a car and it reduced the area for people to get their cars into or out of this parking area. We need to start educating people on the etiquette of driving. This is also another indication of the fact that people do not look or cannot see what is right in front of them.

Many places are now trying to legislate cell phone usage in cars. They cite that this is a distraction to driving. If we are going to consider distractions to driving, we must also consider the general lack of courtesy or respect of other drivers. We must consider the distractions of speed limits that change every few blocks. We must consider the distractions of speed limits that are not appropriate for the road or area. We must consider the distractions of the number of different signs that cities and states are posting along the roads and highways. We must consider the distractions of all the photo and electronic enforcement that many people panic over when they see them. We must consider the distraction of enforcement officers who do not follow the laws or even exhibit the courtesies of good driving practices. We must consider the distraction of all the memorials that people are placing along the road.

Why is it that the government is fully willing to place more distractions and more reasons for people not to pay attention to the road and then turn around and legislate that people cannot have common distractions? Why are they allowed to create all the distractions they want while trying to tell the people to limit their distractions?

It seems interesting, that some of the automobile or driving associations in the past would review areas with bad laws, bad rules, or excessive enforcement, and now they are more interested in selling insurance or credit cards.

Another indication of the advantage of legislation over education is Prohibition. The country tried to legislate against alcohol instead of increasing education. In the process, they created more alcoholics and contributed to the growth of large, corrupt organizations. They also made many people very rich. The failure of their attempt can be seen by the fact that the law had to be repealed.

We continue to use legislation to try to solve problems. We are now trying to legislate against cigarettes. In the process, we hear more and more about how other dangerous drug usage is growing. Again, legislation over education is leading to more and worse problems.

One thing contributing heavily to the problems with legislation is politicians who feel they must show they are doing something. These politicians first think about passing laws, because that is what they do. They have a great need to show they are doing something directly to solve problems. Because they are so focused on the problem, they never consider education, because education is not an immediate solution, and they need to show an immediate solution.

# Homeowners' Associations

Homeowners' associations and their socialistic or communistic rules are a good example of how focusing on what sounds like a good idea can end up creating a nightmare.

The basic idea of a homeowners' association is to protect the value of the properties covered by the association. Along with protecting individual property values, they are also charged with maintaining the common areas such as roads, pools, clubhouses, and tennis courts. Because the idea had some success, it has spread to a large number of subdivisions throughout the country.

One of the things that has made the earlier associations successful was the fact that people who moved to these communities were looking for that kind of a community. These were people were more interested in the pools, clubhouses, tennis courts, golf courses, weight rooms, and social activities that were planned and available for them. These were usually retired people who were outgoing and socially active and liked planned activities. They enjoyed the social interaction and were interested in knowing all their neighbors.

Those who were elected to run these associations usually knew most of the people in their community and probably played tennis or golf with them on a frequent basis. These people all had common interests and desires.

This is similar to what happened early on with HMOs. The people who joined HMOs early on were healthy and did not need a lot of medical attention. Many of them were not worried about the choice of doctors or hospitals because they rarely needed to go to one of them. With this group of people, HMOs were very successful at keeping the costs of medical insurance down. This is what these people were looking for, as they really did not need a lot of attention and felt that they should not have to pay for services they did not need. These people grouped well because of their health needs. The many other factors such as social skills or desires did not enter into the equations.

Both HMOs and homeowners' associations worked well because they were a good fit for the people they served. The people who joined them had very similar needs and desires. They were very compatible.

These were groups of people who, of the millions of traits, desires and needs had a large number of these traits, desires, and needs in common. Therefore they were a good fit to be grouped together and they were able to understand each other's needs and desires.

For HMOs, the important traits were health and little need of health care. Having this group that was not needy for health care meant that these HMOs could keep their costs and premiums down.

As companies that offered health-care insurance started focusing only on the premiums for HMOs (whose rates were much less than other insurance's), they started pressing their employees to move to the HMOs.

As more and more companies pressed more and more employees to convert to HMOs, the dynamics of the needs of these groups changed. There were more people who had more medical needs. That is, there were more people with chronic illnesses that require more doctors and other health-care attention. There were also more people who needed the continual verification from the doctors. With these people with more needs entering HMOs, their cost of services has gone up. With the increase in cost of services going up, the premiums have gone up and are now in many cases similar to traditional insurance providers.

Back to the homeowners' associations. Many developers started focusing on the success of these master-planned communities. They may have even focused on the type of people who were in these master-planned communities.

These developers started developing master-planned communities along with their homeowners' associations in order to compete with the current communities.

With the number of master-planned communities, the numbers of buyers who have similar needs and desires is becoming less and less. And seeing that in many areas you cannot find any new communities that are not master-planned or have a homeowners' association, you are getting a much more diverse group of people entering these communities.

With the greater diversity of owners, you get a greater friction between the owners as to what they want for their neighborhood.

Now let's look at the association rules.

Association rules are usually developed with the idea that they will be used to try to keep the look and quality of the neighborhood much at was when it was developed. In order to keep these rules simple, they are written more in generalities than specifics.

There are rules such as, "You must submit a plan before you do any landscaping or painting, and the association board will make the decision as to if it is acceptable." For those original associations, which attracted people who had many likes and dislikes in common, this really did not create a problem or dissention. But when these types of rules are applied by people who have very few likes and dislikes in common, dissention and friction occur. The more the people are different, the greater the problem becomes.

Now let's focus on a different look at this rule. In Germany in the late 1930s, they were passing laws that basically said that if the government did not like something, it was against the law. This is not much different than the association rules that basically say, "Tell us what you want to do, and we will decide if it is against the rules." And seeing that the rules have very few and vague definitions of what is appropriate, the full decision of what may be done is entirely up to those making the decision.

As I have said, if everyone in the association has a very similar idea of what they want and desire, there will be very little division on what is acceptable.

If you are in an association where there is a wide view of what things should be like, it becomes a roll of the dice if what you want to do will be accepted. If the current association board has similar views to yours, you will probably get your plan approved. If the board members do not share your likes and dislikes, you probably will not get your plan approved.

To take this further, if a board is elected that thinks the association should be very controlling of the owners, they can start imposing the rules as the see fit. In many cases they can force people to change things the board wants changed. These associations now start taking on the traits of socialistic governments where the desires of the few determine how the many must live.

Many examples of this have been in the news in my area.

In one association, a homeowner decided to put Astroturf in his backyard and replace all plant material with artificial flowers and trees. The neighbor had a large tree that had been there for a long time. The homeowner that converted his backyard complained to the homeowners' association that the leaves and dirt from the tree was blowing into his yard and messing up his Astroturf. The association sided with the owner who had converted his yard and ordered the other homeowner to cut down his tree.

Another homeowners' association decided roofs in the neighborhood were getting a little older and ordered all homeowners to immediately have their homes re-roofed.

Other homeowners' associations are using minor violations to levee fines and ultimately accumulating these fines to the point that the association could foreclose on the home and move someone out of the area without any form of legal recourse or judicial review. Of course these fines were determined by a small group of people or even a single person within the association.

There are some associations that are telling the owners they cannot rent their property. This is saying all renters are bad people. If they can do this, can they also say the homeowner cannot sell to specific ethnic groups or those belonging to certain religious groups?

When the homeowners' association in my area sent out a ballot on this, my neighbor thought it was a good idea and had filled out her ballot. Her husband had just passed away, and she was about to put her home on the market. I mentioned to her that by telling people they could not rent the house, they were telling those who might want to buy her house to use for a rental that they could not do that. This meant the number of people interested in buying her home would be reduced. Once she realized that this rule might make selling her home more difficult, she went out to the mailbox, took her ballot back, and changed her vote.

If you only focus on the intentions of homeowners' associations, the ideas are commendable. But if you broaden your view and look past the intentions and look at how different people will apply or use these rules, you realize that you are leaving the door open to abuse, corruption, and demagoguery.

A recent story on TV talked about a homeowners' association that had an owner's daughter's car towed from in front of their house. The car sustained a couple of thousand dollars worth of damage. The daughter was not living there, but she was just visiting for a couple of days. The homeowners' association never gave any warnings and just decided to have the car towed. They also denied they were responsible for any damage to the car. This has now become a legal battle and it looks like the homeowners' association is trying to settle for the damage to the car, but it also looks like that they will be liable also for several more thousands of dollars in legal costs. This means that because of the incompetence of those in charge of the association, all of the homeowners will have to pay for their screw up.

An interesting comment from another resident was that she was glad to see the car towed, because she had small children who played in the street and did not like having cars parked in the street. First, if these are small children, what are they doing playing in the street? The streets were made for cars. Second, later on when these kids grow up and have cars, is she going to have enough room for them to park in her garage, or are they going to end up parking on the street? At that time she will probably be fighting the homeowners' association herself because it is her kids who want to park in the street.

This is another perfect example of people being too focused on what they want at the current time and not having any regard for other people's needs or even on the needs they will have at a different stage of their lives.

I recently saw the monument to the Navajo Code Talkers at Window Rock, Arizona. There is also a memorial to other Native Americans who gave their life defending this country.

This reminded me of the many Americans of all backgrounds who have fought and ultimately gave their lives to give the rest of us a chance at freedom.

These brave Americans fought against those who wanted to impose their ideas and will on us and those in other parts of the world. They fought bravely with the idea that they were eliminating tyrants and oppressors. They fought hard to try to ensure that the people back home would be able to enjoy the freedoms that our Founding Fathers had envisioned for our country.

We, as a people, have done many things to honor the sacrifices of all the people who have served our country. We have dedicated a special day to honor them. We have given many parades to honor them. People put flags and flowers on the graves of the fallen. We have erected monuments and walls of honor for these brave men and women. We have even created shrines out of places were large numbers of them died.

But even with all these honors, I feel that we as a people are doing a great disservice and dishonor to their great sacrifices. We dishonor their effort by allowing laws to be passed that try to limit or control individual freedoms. We allow laws similar to those Hitler was able to get passed—laws that basically say that if those in charge do not like something, it is against the rules or laws. We allow large organizations to push for laws they feel will support their ideas without consideration of other's freedoms. Those who served our country fought against those who felt they and the governments they created were the ones with the only right answers and everyone else should do things their way.

We allow our politicians others to create laws for the "greater good" because it is their idea that their view of the "greater good" is the best for everyone. We are seeing a growing number of groups around the world that are using their religion to push their idea of "the greater good." They are even fighting with other groups who share their religion over whose idea is the right one.

# *Discrimination*

Discrimination is a very pervasive part of the human culture. Discrimination has been around for thousands of years. It has resulted in slavery and oppression throughout history.

Discrimination starts when one person or group of people starts feeling superior to another group. The greater the feeling of superiority, the greater the discrimination becomes.

This feeling of superiority is a form of narcotic. People who start feeling superior to someone else get an adrenaline-type rush. It is a rush to think you are better than someone else. The desire to better oneself leads to a strong feeling when you can feel that you are or have become better than someone else.

The feeling of superiority means that these people lose respect for those they feel are inferior. The more superior a person feels toward someone or some group, the more they feel that person or group is more like an animal than they are a person.

When this feeling of superiority is great enough, they have no problem in treating these others as animals. They feel they can possess them just as they would a cow or a sheep or a pig. They feel these people should only have the rights they give them. They feel these people do not have the right to associate with them or attend any functions they attend. They feel these people are so far inferior that having them around doing anything other than what they are told to do is an insult to their superiority. This leads to the total discrimination against anything that these "lesser" beings might want to have or do.

Religious conversion often leads to a strong adrenaline-type rush. That rush comes with the thought that you have improved your situation. With this rush, people often start feeling superior to those who have not converted.

This is why many people who convert to a religious belief or other social idea tend to become zealots or fanatics. This fanaticism often presents itself as a strong desire to convert other people to their newfound ideas. This need to convert other people is a form of discrimination, in that the new convert feels that he has "moved up" and those who have not seen the light are at a lesser level.

Until those who have not converted see the light, they can never be on an equal plane with the converted. This inequality leads to the feeling that until the unconverted move to this presumed higher plane, these people are not deserving of fully participating in activities that superior people do.

Another form of religious conversion is the conversion to a social idea. This can be seen in the conversions of many people to the fanatical idea of suicide bombers.

These people are bombarded with the idea that others, who do not believe as they do (or should), are inferior and do not deserve to live. This is one of the most extreme examples of discrimination.

Even though these ideas are supposedly based on some religious belief, someone or some group trying to advance their control is usually perverting this belief. This can be seen by the fact that many of these suicide bombers are a not just attacking people outside their religion. They are also attacking those within the religion they are supposed to be supporting.

These people are again discriminating against people who do not believe exactly as they do or as those who are controlling them do. If you do not do as we want, you are of no importance, and if you are not important to us, your life is only useful in helping us succeed in our desires.

Discrimination is basically a tool to promote someone's feeling of superiority and idea of right, wrong, or position.

Let's take a look at a recent example—the attack on smokers. There are a lot of people who feel superior to smokers. They do not look at smokers as rational or intelligent people. They feel smokers are inferior to them and should therefore not have equal rights.

There is another group—those who have quit smoking. This gives them the feeling of superiority because they have been able to kick the habit. (I would like to know how many of them have turned to other drugs to take the place of the cigarettes.) Many of them have become "born-again" non smokers. They think that because they have quit smoking, everyone should up and do the same.

We also have those in the medical communities who have spent years studying smoking and all its effects on the human body. While these folks have been focusing on this one topic, I believe they have not allowed themselves to look at any data outside of what they want to focus on. This can be seen in many cases where two different studies run by people with opposite views come up with very different conclusions from the same data.

With all this focus on how bad smoking is and the feeling of superiority that has been developed among those opposed to smoking, it is inevitable that discrimination will follow.

There are several examples of this. One is that business owners do not have the right to run their business as they choose. They do not have the right to make their own decision as to whether they can allow smoking in their establishment. The people who do business at these places do not have the right to choose if they wish to continue doing business with an establishment that allows smoking.

Those who feel superior to smokers are voting for taxes on cigarettes. They feel their superiority gives them the right to take money from smokers and give it to the politicians to do with what they want. They also feel that because they are superior to smokers, they can discriminate against them by making smokers pay for projects they want instead of taxing themselves to fund these projects.

It also appears they feel smoking is more dangerous than other drugs. In many cases, the punishment for smoking is more severe than for smoking pot or taking other illegal drugs.

Even though discrimination for many reasons has been made illegal in this country, discrimination for all sorts of things is growing. There is discrimination against whole groups of people because people feel superior to those few in the groups who misuse or abuse something common to that group.

There is discrimination against cell phone users. There is discrimination against gun owners. There is discrimination against classes of people. There is discrimination against the poor. There is discrimination against car buyers and drivers. There is discrimination against truck drivers, et cetera.

If people feel superior to people who do things they do not like, they start discriminating against them. They start looking for ways to make rules and laws that support their superiority. By doing this, they are creating more discrimination.

# Why Do Descendants of Slaves Vote for Slavery?

In the history of our country, we have had slaves from many areas of the world. In fact, if we look deeply into the current plight of our country, we will probably find instances of slavery are still occurring.

What is it that causes the descendants of those who were forced into slavery to be so susceptible to political slavery?

How can I say this when these people have been freed? The political leaders that many of these people turn to are telling them that the government owes them for their plight. These leaders are using this to focus them on their agenda and thus gain their support. These are "hooks" to draw them in and make the people think that politicians are really interested in their plight and that they want the government to help make amends for the wrong that was allowed.

Let's take a look at the types of programs they have and are proposing and what the actual results are—programs such as public housing, public health care, public assistance, and so on.

Public housing projects have been around for quite some time. In fact, in many places they have been called "the projects." These have had a sordid history. They were used as a reason to tear down what was perceived as blighted areas of many cities. They were also used to give fat contracts to developers. (Could this have helped gain support for the politicians?)

Once these projects were built, there needed to be a bureaucracy to identify who should get into and subsequently manage these buildings. As with many government bureaucracies that are usually under funded, many of the people in them are not the best qualified or most compassionate people. For the most part, more-qualified people are able to find better and more rewarding jobs in the private sector. Also, dealing with the people who are eligible for these types programs can be very trying and draining. These potential recipients are frequently quite stressed and overwhelmed by their lives and circumstances. This can make them more challenging to work with and can be draining on those bureaucrats who must deal with them.

With this in mind, it is no wonder that these bureaucrats may feel overwhelmed and stressed. In order to cope with this and to feel like they are important, their personality at work starts changing and they feel they must control the people they are there to help. They also start feeling the power they have in their position. They feel that they can control the lives of those they are there to help. They have the power as to whether people get in or not. They have the power to determine if they can stay. They have the power to determine where in the project they can live. This scenario is starting to sound a little like slavery.

The bureaucrats are also in charge of maintaining these projects. They have a limited amount of funds to do maintenance and security. As time goes on, the politicians, having seen their projects built and reaped the maximum political benefit, start deciding that some of the funds to maintain these properties could be used to better advantage somewhere else. This change in funding can also be attributed to new politicians getting into power and having different priorities for the funds. This means that maintenance and security on these properties begins to suffer. With these things starting to suffer, crime and drug use increases. This moves the people living there back toward the blight they were expecting to get out of.

Now the politicians again have the opportunity to start over, clearing the blight and convincing the people they are going to help them and to create large contracts for correcting the problem. This again will put the people they are trying to help back into a position of having their lives controlled by bureaucrats.

Another thing about public housing is that by helping people pay rent, they also help keep them dependent on the government. The people do not gain anything to help them become independent. The money does not build any equity except for those who own the public housing. It is interesting that organizations such as Habitat for Humanity are better able to understand this than our politicians are. This organization is helping people to have a home of their own, and their payments are building equity for their future. This not only gives them a place to live, but it also gives them hope and a way to a better future.

Another big idea is assistance to the poor. This again will require contracts for facilities to run the assistance programs and large numbers of bureaucrats to run the assistance programs. These bureaucrats will run into the same problems and situations as those running the projects. They will also have the power to determine who, what, and how the people will receive assistance. This again puts someone in control the lives of these people.

Many assistance programs are supposedly designed to get people out of their predicament—to get them out from under the control of the bureaucrats and out on their own, controlling their own lives.

These programs are supposed to give training and education to make the recipient self-sufficient. At the same time, they are giving help with living expenses. After a period of time, the people are to move off of the program and be able to support themselves. Many who go through these programs did it so they could, indeed, get out of the projects and get out of their situation. The problem is that many of these do give job training and job skills, but these people will have to move off of public assistance to low-paying, entry-level jobs. These jobs in many cases are not going to pay the person enough to replace the help they are getting from the government. Also, many have children and will need daycare. If they take the job, they will have to move off of assistance, and they will end up in a worse situation. As with many government projects, there is no end game in the plan. There is little or no appropriate transitional support to allow time for or help while a person tries to work their way out of the entry-level job.

This has also contributed to the fact that we now are dealing with second and third generations of families living under governmental programs.

This means that many people who truly want to get out from under control of the government are not given the proper help they need to do it. There is an up side to this. These people remain dependent on the government and remain dependent on those politicians that say they are going to help them.

These programs will require the controlling of large amounts of money, large bureaucracies, and have the added benefit of giving people the hope they will be helped. These are the lifeblood of politicians.

In the light of the current political fight over the handling of the war in Iraq, I find it interesting that many of the politicians who are so in favor of these types of social programs are the most vocal about establishing an end game for Iraq. If they are so knowledgeable about how to end that war, why have they not been able to create a real end strategy to get these people out from under governmental programs?

# Overall Attack on the Poor

People are talking about how the division between the classes is widening. The rich are getting richer and the poor are getting poorer. They keep talking about the fact that this is happening, but no one seems to be talking about how or why. They seem to think that just by bringing up the subject, something magical will happen to correct this problem.

One factor that contributes to the number of poor people is a person's ability. I am not talking about a person's self-imposed limits on their ability. What I am talking about are those physical and mental disabilities that may limit a person's ability to better their situation.

Many people with some form of disability have the ability to improve their situation. They may not be able to achieve everything a person without disabilities can, but there usually are many things they are able to do. People who have lost the use of their legs may not be able to run a marathon. But there are many people who have lost the use of their legs who have entered marathons in wheelchairs. These are groups of people who have found a way to improve their position and reach a goal. This may not have been the ultimate goal they wanted, but it is a goal far above what they might have felt they could achieve.

There are a few people who do have disabilities that cannot be overcome. Unfortunately, many of those who have disabilities that can be overcome become limited by their perception of what they can do. These people are often further limited and held back by misdirected people around them and a misdirected government that thinks they should take over their lives.

These are the people who through no fault of their own will remain among the poorest in America.

Another large problem keeping the poor class poor is education. There are several causes of this.

Family structure and values are a large contributor to the lack of educational opportunities among the poor. Living in a poor or undereducated family tends to perpetuate poor and undereducated families. These families usually do not see or understand the value of education. They tend not to stress or support the education of their children.

Politicians and bureaucrats also have a large responsibility in the undereducation of the poor. Having the poor to cater to gives them some emotional and political gain. They can use anything they do for the poor as a leverage to get votes. It does not necessarily have to be something that can help them to get out of their situation.

The problem for politicians is that education is not something that has an immediate result. If they help fund a soup kitchen, fund housing, or fund food stamps, they have something that they can show as an immediate help. Education and helping families get their children educated is something does not show immediate results. They seem to think that "giving a person a fish instead of teaching them to fish" is much better for their position. People can immediately see them giving the "fish."

There are many poor people who are doing all the right things trying to get out of their situation. They are working hard. They are trying to get their children educated. They are doing their best to keep a home (not just a house).

The problem is that these people cannot quite get to what I call the "critical mass" to get out of their situation. This is to get to the income level so that they can start saving some money. Part of this is the fact that they do not have enough money to take advantage of things like being able to by food in quantities that will save them money.

An example of this is coffee. I have been watching the price of the coffee I buy. The price is usually between nine to twelve dollars. I have seen it on sale at five to six dollars. When it is on sale at this price, I usually buy two or three cans. This means that when I run out of coffee, I do not have to buy it at the higher price, thus saving me several dollars.

An interesting aside on this example is that I hear a lot of people say that the rich have so many more opportunities to make money. Using the above, if coffee is normally selling for nine dollars and it is on sale for six dollars, you save three dollars on the can you need right now. If you, for example, use four cans of coffee a year and you buy a second can, let's calculate the return on investment on that second can. If in three months when you need the next can it is back to nine dollars, you have saved again three dollars. This is a 50 percent return on your six-dollar investment in three months. This is a return on your investment of over 200 percent on an annualized basis. Most wealthy people are working with returns on their money that is in most cases not much better than 10 to 20 percent on an annualized basis. One of the differences is that the more wealthy people will take their savings and reinvest it in other opportunities.

For the poor people who are struggling to even put food on the table, they do not have the extra funds (critical mass) to buy the second can of coffee. This means that when they run out of coffee, they will probably have to buy it at the higher price, thus costing them the extra several dollars they could have used for something else.

While I am using coffee as an example because it is something that I personally watch, this same scenario applies to many other things in the stores.

The politicians have set up many programs for the poor. As I have said, these include such things as housing, daycare, and training programs. Many of these programs become self-perpetuating. While they do give help to many people, many, if not most, of these programs do not have an end game. They may help bring people up from a very serious situation, but they usually fall short of getting them anywhere near that critical mass. These programs usually get them to a point that they are off the program, but it is not up to a sustainable level. This means that these people will probably fall back on to these programs.

After people have made attempts to get off these programs, only to keep falling back, they will finally stop trying and just play the system and remain on the programs.

These people then become so dependent on these programs that they become very vulnerable to manipulation by politicians who are most likely to continue or expand these programs.

Taxes and fees and fines are among the biggest things that keep people poor. As I have said, there are many people working hard to better themselves but who are not quite able to reach the critical mass.

While most income taxes are graduated in accordance to the person's income, most other taxes, fees, and fines are not. They are a one-size-fits-all type of assessment.

I do not know if the politicians who put these assessments in place are so blind to this fact that they do not understand this or if they do understand it and want to keep this constituency dependent on them.

Let's start with sales tax. This is a flat tax that has no regard with a person's ability to pay. Many places do not tax food because everyone, both rich and poor, needs food. But both the rich and poor need other things like clothing, utilities, housing, and transportation.

In my area, sales tax is running about 8 percent. This means that a family of four who would have to spend one to two hundred dollars on shoes in a year would pay between eight to sixteen dollars in tax just on those shoes. This could be several days of food for many poor families. For many others and me, this is not much more than a nuisance or irritation. For some others, they may not even think about it.

For the poor, this is another thing that keeps them from getting to the critical mass where they can start to take full advantage of sales and quantity buying.

Other than farmers and some business owners who live above their stores, most people have to travel to their work. Most of those people have to travel distances that are too far to walk or even ride a bicycle. And for the poorer people who are working multiple jobs, the time it would take to walk or ride a bike would be taken from needed time with their family or sleep.

With this in mind, it becomes evident that these people need cars or public transportation. Most public transportation does not cover the needs of these people. It either does not go where they need or does not go there when they need it.

This means that they either need a car or they need to find someone to share a ride with. In either case this transportation comes with fees and taxes.

There are sales taxes on the vehicle. There are driver license fees. There are automobile license fees. There are federal, state, and local fuel taxes. Again, these fees and taxes do not discriminate against a person's class, but they do indeed punish or hurt the poorest people the most. These again help prevent these people from reaching the critical mass to get out of their plight.

Now that they have a car, they are under the peril of being ticketed for some type of violation. You can say that if they would follow the rules, they would not have to worry about this. I do not know of anyone who has been driving for any length of time who has not received a traffic citation at some time in their driving career. And now with the electronic or photo enforcement I have discussed, the probability is even higher, even if the person has not done anything wrong. Most of these tickets have a fine well in excess of $150. This amount is extremely discriminatory to the poor. This cannot only prevent some of these people from reaching the critical mass, but it can also force some to fall back into a bleaker future. They may even have to fall back on public assistance of some form or other.

Another thing these people need is housing. They are probably renters and included in the rent is the owner's payments of property tax. If any of these people are lucky enough to be able to get a home through organizations such as Habitat for Humanity, they will still have to pay the same rate of property tax as their neighbors who may have better jobs and more income.

Recently in the town I live in, there has been a proposal to put a tax on rentals to pay for a pet transportation project of the politicians in the town. One of the newspapers in the area said, "A proposed transaction privilege tax on residential and commercial rentals may be the means that the town will use to put itself ahead of the curve in regard to public transportation." Here again is the media hyping and supporting the views of the politicians without ever reviewing or considering the downside or negative aspects. They too seem not to be interested in the plight of the poorer members of our society. If they were actually performing the duties of the fourth estate and helping to protect the interests of the people they serve, they would have posed questions on the negative aspects of this tax. They would have pointed out that almost all of the poor people are forced by their position to rent their dwellings. They would also have pointed out that the owners of these rentals, like any other business or government, will have to pass these costs on to the renters and thus to those who can least afford it. This is not much different than the politicians raising their pay and then raising the taxes to pay for it.

In any case, the resultant cost will be disproportionately felt by the poor. Of course, this again gives politicians another chance to say they need to raise other taxes to help the poor because they are becoming less able to afford their rents. Of course they can't afford their rents, because the politicians are causing them to go up. Where does this stop? Isn't anyone looking or listening? Where is the fourth estate that is supposed to be looking out for the welfare of the people and questioning the politicians?

All of these taxes, fees, and fines have been decided on by politicians without regard to the effect they have on the different classes.

As I have said, I do not know if this is because of ignorance or they just don't care or if it is by design. In any case, their actions are having a definite influence on the divide between the classes. And this influence on the divide is having the greatest effect on the poorest among us.

# Global Warming

While I do not disagree with the fact that global warming may be happening, I do think there are many things that should be questioned and considered. Among them is the need to watch the money.

The main reason that I feel that this is important is that many of the causes and solutions being put forth will generate billions or trillions of dollars of opportunity. With dollar amounts like these at stake, politicians and businesspeople sit up and take notice. Not only do they take notice, but they also start looking for ways to get an advantage. They start generating spin to get an advantage. And, with this amount of money at stake, I do not see how greed and corruption can be kept out. Given these facts, it is important that we question the conclusions being put forth. It would also be nice if the news media, when they are reporting on these conclusions, would also raise some questions as to the validity of the conclusion. This needs to be done not only by special reports or programs but also as part of the ten-second sound bites that most of the people get their information from.

Something that needs to be watched for is how much of the global warming is coming from human causes and how much is coming from natural causes. I say this because if people can say that something is being done by the people, they can use this to generate ideas and business from. Let's just make sure the facts support this.

One prominent cause being put forth is the emissions from cars. By saying this, there are many companies racing to cash in on this. They talk about wanting to reduce emissions by X percent in the next Y years. I do not hear anything about the fact that when that time comes, there will be so many more cars added that the net effect will be an increase in the emissions. The car companies won't be unhappy to hear this because this will mean more opportunity for them, so they do not want this to be publicized.

An interesting thing I heard on the news is that the UN has released a report that seems to indicate that the greenhouse gasses emitted from raising animals for food is more than that produced by all the vehicles, boats, and planes in the world.

While this does not mean that the pollution from these vehicles is not important, it does mean that when people are talking about cutting greenhouse gasses in half by reducing emissions from vehicles, they are spinning the numbers. If more than half of the greenhouse gasses are not from vehicles, if you eliminated all the pollution from vehicles, you still would not cut the greenhouse gasses in half.

I heard that at the recent G8 summit, there was talk about cutting some emissions by 50 percent in a little over forty years. I figure that given population growth, there will be roughly three times as many people on this planet. In order to achieve a 50 percent reduction from today's numbers, it is an actual 83 percent reduction per person over today's rates. This means the emissions caused by every person must be reduced to a little over 16.5 percent. There are many developing countries such as China where people are getting richer and therefore are using more things that contribute to these emissions. This then reduces the 16.5 percent considerably. I do not know how much, but one thing that does strike me is that more than 50 percent of current emissions per person come from growing animals for food. So if 50 percent of our current emissions per person come from food production, how are we to reduce our emissions to less than 16.5 percent per person? Is anyone expected to need food?

Why do I say that this will occur? Because the population of this country and the world is growing that fast. This is not a surprise to many people. Why do politicians seem to ignore this and only give it lip service? It is because more people mean more taxes and being able to control more people means more power. Also, another problem may be the religious ramifications of any attempt to control population growth.

Currently, China is the only country that I know of that has taken strong action to try to control population growth. I am not trying to make any judgment on how they are doing it, just that they are making an attempt to do something that will have an actual effect on it.

Here in the United States and in many other countries, politicians may be giving lip service to overpopulation as a problem while the government is subsidizing the having of children. We give tax credits for having children and for things like daycare. While these may not be all bad, why is there not a limit on the number of children per family that these credits apply to? I have heard that if the average family has 2.4 children, the population would stabilize. Above that the population grows and less than that the population would decrease. Why have all of our politicians been so quiet about this and why have they not at least tried to start reducing the subsidies that support the problem of overpopulation?

As I have said, I do not disagree with the fact that the world is going through a warming period. This has been known for many decades. What I am interested in is seeing that the people get and understand the real facts and that partial facts are not used to promote someone's private agenda, or that facts are twisted to line someone's pocket at the people's expense.

Let's remember that at one time this whole world was a molten mass in space or that at one point the whole world was covered with ice. The world has an underlying rhythm of change and this cannot be attributed to people.

Let's look at some natural events that are adding heat to the exterior of the planet.

It is interesting that I recently saw a commercial on television that mentioned an island where thirty-two acres of land were being created each year from a lava flow. This lava had to build from the sea floor, meaning that there is quite a volume of hot material heating the water and the air. While in global terms this in itself may not be a great amount of heat.

We know a lot about the climate of the world above the land and the sea. The ocean has been considered the last frontier. This may be true, and we are still learning what is in the ocean and what goes on under its surface. We are finding that there are many hot vents or underwater volcanoes. I am sure that there are many more that have not been found yet. Also, there are no historical maps that show those vents we are finding nor any technical information that can be used to determine if there is more or less heat being released by those we know about.

Remember that the earth is not a solid ball. It has a liquid molten center that has convection currents and is continually but slowly moving. This center, more than likely, has areas that are hotter or colder than others. If these areas start changing places, this would start to affect the areas above them.

Another thing to remember is that a lot of the weather is controlled by the oceans. Something to think about is that the saltier the ocean is, the higher temperature difference must be to create evaporation. For millions of years water has been evaporating from the ocean and falling as rain on the land. As this pure water runs across the land and rocks, it leaches out salts and minerals. This water then runs back to the sea, only to be evaporated again. When this happens, it leaves behind the minerals that it had leached from the land. This means that the seas should be getting saltier. With this the temperature of the water will climb to allow evaporation. Also, the many vents under the oceans are also adding minerals to the water. All of this has been adding mineral content to the oceans for many years, and it is causing the ocean to slowly getting warmer.

In recent times, the magnetic north pole has been moving away from the geographical north pole, and it is moving at an increased rate. This would indicate that the core, which is made up of liquid iron and other magnetic metals, is probably moving or rotating. This again could mean that the hot and cold areas of the core are moving. This could be causing different amounts of heat in different areas of the crust of the earth.

The crust under many parts of the ocean is thinner and if these changes are occurring in the core, it could contribute to more hot vents and lava flows under the sea. As we do not have a detailed map of hot vents or lava flows, we cannot be sure there haven't been more of them appearing.

Another item I have heard is that there is or was an area in Antarctica that in some winters would be frozen solid and in other winters would go through the winter as a lake. There is supposedly an experiment where a thermos of water was put in a freezer with a small heating element in the bottom. The water at the surface would alternately freeze solid and thaw to liquid. While I am not trying to say the crust will liquefy, the innermost area of the crust could be alternating be getting thicker and thinner.

In recent history, we have developed a network of thermometers and ways of determining the temperature on the surface, in the atmosphere, and to a much lesser extent at various depths in the oceans. We do not have the same capability of knowing the temperature throughout the depths of the crust. Given this, and the fact that the history of actual temperatures in the air and water, there is no way to truly understand if the heat flow from the core has changed or how much it has changed or where it has changed. These changes could have a profound effect on the global temperature.

While I am on the subject of Antarctica, another thing that was major news a few years ago is the hole in the ozone layer, which everyone was so sure was going to be the end of human life on earth. At the time there was a large area that appeared to have a reduced level of ozone. In reading some information on this, I discovered that the ozone-hole phenomenon had only been discovered in the 1980s. The first thing that comes to my mind is that we are trying to predict what was going to happen over a long time based on a very short period of information. Also in recent years, scientists have been able to determine from ice core samples that there had been periods in the history of Antarctica during which the ozone layer had substantially thinned or disappeared several times in the past.

It is interesting that for about a year there did not seem to be a week that went by that there was not a story in the news about the growing hole in the ozone layer. Toward the end of this period, I did some checking of my own and found that the one large hole they were talking about had developed into two holes that totaled only about half of the area. The amount of coverage seemed to dwindle as the area of the hole decreased. I haven't heard anyone talking about the ozone hole with regard to the current global warming or catastrophe problems.

This is another case of people trying to use information based on, in global time, a very short time to make long-range predictions on natural fluctuations. Why would they put so much hype into their "discoveries"? Well, my opinion is that politicians and people with vested interests are trying to use these discoveries to scare the people so that they can push their agenda and/or to profit from some perceived solution to the problem. Money seems to always be a good reason to push limited information of perceived impending disaster.

The news recently reported that astronomers are seeing solar flares that are a factor or factors of ten times greater than they have seen before. These are large jets of hot gas shooting great distances from the surface of the sun. These flares are putting a very hot heat source closer to the earth. These could be contributing to an unexpected increase of heat to our atmosphere.

All of these and other factors and probably many others could be contributing to global warming. We could be in the middle of an unusual number of events all happening at the same time.

All of this is not to diminish the problem of global warming. Also, this is not to say that man is not contributing to global warming also.

What I am trying to say is that there are many variables involved in the equation. Given the number of variables, we need to learn what the impact of any of them is compared to the others. Without this type of information, it will be very easy for unscrupulous people and politicians to exaggerate a cause to achieve political or financial gain. We need to thoroughly examine things before we spend enormous amounts of money or make changes in our lives because of something we may not be able to change or affect.

People are talking about the melting of the Arctic glaciers. They say this is being caused by manmade problems. I found the following on the web at http://ga.water.usgs.gov/edu/earthglacier.html.

Ice and Glaciers Come and Go

There are many long-term weather patterns that the Earth goes through. The climate, on a global scale, is always changing, although usually not at a rate fast enough for people to notice. There have been many warm periods, such as when the dinosaurs lived and many cold periods, such as the last ice age of about 20,000 years ago. During the last ice age much of the northern hemisphere was covered in ice and glaciers, and they covered nearly all of Canada, much of northern Asia and Europe, and extended well into the United States.

This glacier covered the north central United States and is credited with creating the Great Lakes. The current glaciers in North America are remnants of this ice sheet. This ice sheet has been melting for some twenty thousand years, and I do not think man has been the cause of this.

Recently the news covered a man who jumped into the twenty-eight-degree water at the North Pole and swam for a few minutes. The idea of this was to draw attention to the perceived global warming. He was said to have been swimming in an area that in the past had been covered year-round in ice. I find it interesting that the media did not also show the thousands of people who swim in Lake Michigan off of Chicago. These people are also swimming in a body of water that was at one time under a mile of ice year-round. In fact, this was part of the same ice sheet that covered the area that he was swimming in.

While I do not deny humans are causing changes in the climate, I do not feel that those changes are as great people would have you think. The normal cycles of the climate cannot be denied as being an extremely strong force far greater than man. I have heard somewhere that at one point after the Ice Age, there was an estimate that the global temperature went up ten degrees in a matter of a few decades.

Again, we need to be careful about jumping to conclusions and rushing to spend billions of dollars because someone is spinning the numbers to indicate we are the major cause of climate change.

People are talking about the global warming as occurring because of recent history. One thing to remember is that the longest daylight in the northern hemisphere occurs in late June. One would think that with the sun being up for the longest hours at this time, this would be the hottest day of the year. As we all know, the hottest weather occurs after that date. The time from July through September is the hottest time of the year. This indicates that the heating occurs much later than the peak solar heating day. Would this not also hold true for global warming? Would not the effects of the warming become apparent long after the causes started it? This means the major causes for our current warming probably occurred many years ago. This condition, like the summer heat, is not just the result of current conditions but also of some condition that occurred in the past. Given the fact that the climate change has been occurring for more than twenty thousand years, since ice covered much of North America, how can we say the conditions we are now experiencing are the result of some recent changes and not a culmination of factors set in motion hundreds of years ago? This would be well before the influences of man.

Another example I recently heard on a news show is that the movie *An Inconvenient Truth* talks about the melting snow on Mount Kilimanjaro. They were saying that ever since the snows were first seen, they have been melting. They commented that the snow was known to be melting long before many of the chemicals people say are causing it were discovered. Again, people are spinning the numbers to create the sensationalism needed to promote their agenda.

Here is an excerpt from a CNN story. "Most of the retreat occurred before 1953, nearly two decades before any conclusive evidence of atmospheric warming was available ..."

Also, another article says that the snowcap is not "melting." It says that the snow is subliming or in essence, evaporating. This means it is going directly from snow or ice to vapor.

Global warming, along with the passing of all the controlling laws, is an outgrowth of a societal change that has occurred. We have become what I like to call a microwave society. Just like the microwave has allowed us to have "instant" meals, we are looking for instant answers to everything. We think of global warming and its causes as something that is happening in an instant and that instant is indicative of the millions of years the earth has been here. We also look at passing laws similarly. We think we can solve the problems that have plagued man since the beginning of time by passing laws that will instantly solve the problem. We think that by passing laws, we have put the problem in the microwave and it will be done in an instant.

Right now there is a large push for alternative fuels. People have been talking about how much money the oil companies have been making, and now with this push for alternative fuels, there are many opportunities for people to make a killing. There are not going to be large amounts to be made in creating these fuels, but these projects will also cause a large ripple effect into many areas of our life.

Let's take a look at the current drive to create ethanol from corn. First of all, the farmers are facing increasing demand for corn. With this increased demand, the price of corn has been going up. This will help many of the small farmers who have been struggling. It will be an even greater boon to those many large corporate farms. I am sure there is a great probability that some of this money is going back into supporting those who are pushing this project.

Now that the price of corn is going up, the price of other products that depend on corn are going up. Beef, pork, and poultry prices are going up as well as other products, such as milk and eggs. As with most businesses, these businesses work on a profit margin. This means that as the prices go up, the same percentage of profit margin means that they make more money on the same amount of product. I am not saying that the profit margin is a bad thing. All business works on some form of profit margin to maintain profitability. This does favor those who have been in business for a longer time, because a lot of their initial costs have already been fixed, and they are not going up.

Another thing whose price will start to rise is that of farmland. Farmers are going to be looking for more land to plant corn, and with the demand and price for corn going up, they will be willing and able to pay more for the land. This will also affect the price of land for homes.

Another commodity that will be affected is something few people have probably even thought of. That commodity is water. The increase in the number of acres of corn that will be grown will require a larger increase in water usage. There are many areas that do not need extensive extra water to grow the corn. As the demand for corn increases, more areas that require more watering are going to be planted. Many parts of the country are going through moderate to severe drought situations. This will put an added strain on these limited water supplies. Because of this, the cost of water will rise as water districts search for and tap into more expensive water resources. This could even mean areas will have to turn to things such as desalinization to meet the demand. These desalinization plants and the need to move water longer distances will require more energy to run.

Another factor to consider is the fact that gallon for gallon, from what I am hearing, these fuels do not produce as much energy as that from gasoline. This means that a vehicle will not travel as far on a gallon of ethanol as it would on a gallon of gasoline. If the price of a gallon of ethanol is the same as that of a gallon of gasoline, the per-mile cost of driving will increase. This means if you only get 80 percent of the mileage, the actual of cost of the fuel is 125 percent of the price you see on the pump.

For years the government has required that fuels be rated by octane level, which is some indication as to how well your car will run and what kind of mileage you will get from a gallon. I think that there should be a new rating system for fuels that would be more indicative of what kind of mileage can be expected from the fuel. This should be done in such a way that the average person can estimate how much it will cost to run his vehicle per mile. For example, with the current grades in fuel, it might be more economical for some vehicles to use a more expensive grade of gasoline. That is to say that the driver may get more miles for the same dollars by using a higher grade of gasoline. Yes, the cheaper grade of gasoline may be costing people more money.

As we can see, there are many other things whose costs are going up in order to be able to produce this alternative fuel. This means that we are not only paying the price for this fuel at the pump, but we are also paying for this fuel in the increased prices of other products. This means the price we see at the pump does not reflect the true cost of the fuel as it is with our current oil prices.

With all the billions of dollars all the different aspects of this alternative fuel will generate, let's try to make sure there will be an actual benefit to the people. Let's make sure it is not going to just generate huge profits for small groups of people while we end up in a worse situation. Let's not just focus on the fact that we are replacing oil, but let's also make sure we are actually solving the problem.

Many of those who are pressing the global warming problem are pushing for more fuel-efficient cars. One of the biggest hurdles in increasing the efficiency of cars is the laws of physics. There are physical limits on how much fuel it will take to accelerate or move a given amount of mass.

People who keep saying there are carburetors that oil companies are hiding that will make cars go fifty or one hundred miles on a gallon of gasoline do not understand physics. I am sure someone will find ways to make cars more efficient by changing the carburetion process. But these improvements will be very small and nowhere near the improvement some say is possible. The laws of physics say that these numbers are impossible.

The only way to make those kinds of gains in fuel usage is to make the cars smaller and lighter. The amount of fuel per mile is directly proportional to the amount of mass that must be moved. The less mass, the less fuel. There are several problems with smaller cars. People with families need to have room to carry those families. This means those one- and two-person mini-cars are impractical for them. People who travel need room for their luggage and other things they may need on trips. Salespeople need to have room to carry their samples and other wares to show their customers. Real estate salespeople need room to take their clients around to show properties.

While conservationists are right when they say that if everyone drove around in those small individual vehicles, it would make a difference in fuel consumption, but as you can see, these vehicles are not practical for everyone or every occasion. People could buy these small vehicles for their individual trips, but they would also need the larger vehicles for their other usages. But not everyone can afford to have multiple vehicles for special purposes and all the extra fuel that would be needed to make all these extra vehicles would probably be more than what they would save.

Another side problem to the higher mileage and electric cars is that people do not need to stop as often for fuel. If you are like me, I need to have a restroom break every so often. On the freeways, there are rest stops out away from towns, but in the cities and on the other highways, there are few or none. With cars going farther before needing fuel, gas station owners are getting rather upset at people stopping just to use the restrooms and not purchasing fuel. Many are now closing their restrooms to the public. Federal and state governments are going to need to do something about this by either putting up more public restrooms or, as they have done in some areas, helping to subsidize restrooms in service stations. The government also needs to put up more signs to let travelers know where these restrooms can be found.

On a recent trip, I avoided the freeways and took some of the back highways, as it was not only shorter, but it also gave us the opportunity to see some very pretty scenery. In the several hundred miles I traveled on these "back roads," I only saw one public restroom, and I did not even know it was there until after we passed it. We did stop at a gas station, but the people there were not too pleased with us using their restroom. In a way I cannot blame them. I did not need much gas.

# Gun Control

Another good example of focusing on the world through two toilet paper tubes on a pair of glasses is gun control. People and politicians have become overly focused on the gun as the root of all evil. A gun by itself does not kill or harm people. It is only when we introduce the human element that a gun becomes a danger to other people.

This does not mean that all human-gun interactions are dangerous or harmful. There are many people who enjoy having guns as a hobby. They enjoy disassembling, cleaning, and re-assembling them. There are many who enjoy going to a range and shooting targets. They enjoy the challenge of trying to place bullets in the center of a target. To them this is not much different than a golfer trying to make a hole in one. By the way, golf clubs have been used to injure and kill people also.

Many gun owners enjoy going hunting for game to use as food. This gets them out of their everyday life and into the open country. It can give them an opportunity to get away from a stressful existence and do something completely different, thus giving them time to relax. If you wish to focus on the fact that they are killing something, it would be good to remember that everything we eat was at sometime living and growing.

One good example of focusing on finding a marginal way to control a problem is the way we have tried to implement gun control. The Constitution gives the citizens of the United States the right to bear arms. The Founding Fathers felt that citizens in good standing had the right to protect themselves.

Since politicians could not make owning a gun illegal, they implemented gun registration and waiting periods. Requiring registration gives the government information to use against the people. With guns being registered, if the government decides to try to further make guns illegal by making a certain type of gun illegal, they now know where to look.

This gives them a reason to enter any home where one of these guns is registered. In other words, they now have the laws to violate the sanctity of a person's home for having something that was legal. To me, this not only violates a person's right to bear arms, but it also violates the laws of search and retroactively making something illegal, which is also against the Constitution.

I heard a story that relates to this about a man who moved to another state. He had a gun and inquired about registering it. He was told there would be no problem and that he should register it. Shortly after registering it, the police came to his door and confiscated the weapon, saying that it was an illegal weapon. This is a good example of how registration gives the government the ability to identify those who have guns and rapidly be able to confiscate them.

As to waiting periods, I had a friend, Dennis, who owned several handguns he enjoyed using for target practice. If he decided he wanted a different type or caliber of gun to use for his hobby, he to had to register and go through the waiting period. This waiting period is supposedly imposed to keep someone from being able to buy a gun and immediately go out and commit a crime. First, Dennis was not a criminal and only wanted the gun for his hobby. Second, if he wanted a gun to commit a crime, he only had to go to his gun safe and choose from his selection of guns.

This is not only an example of attempts to take away rights that are given to us in the Constitution, but this is also an example of the government punishing the average honest and hard-working citizen by interfering with him going about his life.

Another interesting thought that the crafters of the Bill of Rights had when they gave the citizens the right to bear arms is that they felt the people should not fear the government; instead the government should fear the people. They felt the people had the right to protect their rights. They felt if the populace was armed, it would be more difficult for a tyrannical government to get control. Today, the government appears to be trying to protect themselves from the populace and does not want them to have access to guns. They only want those organizations they control and that support them to have weapons.

Does gun control really protect the average person? From what I have read, there does not seem to be any definitive results that show any significant support for this idea.

There are many news stories that seem to show that gun control only adds to the problem. We hear of criminals who have many guns and none of them are registered. They have either stolen them from people who have them or found some illegal source, such as personal guns, gun stores, police stations, or armories. They have also obtained them from other criminals who have smuggled them into the country.

I guess what I am really trying to point out is that criminals are not going to be stopped from having weapons by the requirement for registration or if a particular gun has been made illegal. After all, they are criminals, and the law does not encumber them. The make their own rules and laws.

Given this fact, the only people who are really affected by gun control laws are the average, decent citizens. Are these really the ones the government is worried about?

Several news stories, recent and past, tend to show what happens when the average person is limited from having or carrying a gun.

One of the first that comes to mind is a shooting of several individuals of various ethnic backgrounds in Los Angeles several years ago. The gunman, as I remember, shot several people in a Jewish center in Los Angeles and then started shooting other people of various ethnic backgrounds. Among them was a postman on his rounds. After he was captured, it was determined that he lived in Washington state and had come to Los Angeles specifically to do the shootings. When he was asked why he came to Los Angeles to do his shooting, he said that it was safer for him to do it there. He said the people in Washington state had guns, and he was worried that someone might shoot him. He knew that there were far less guns in Los Angeles, and he was far less likely to be shot.

Another story comes from England, where there is very strong gun control. They had an incident where someone with a gun was able to open fire on a group of school children. He probably felt safe in doing this because even the police there were not allowed to carry guns.

Another interesting story comes from England during World War II. I heard that Winston Churchill is quoted as saying that he was worried about the Germans coming across the channel and invading England. He was worried because England had strict gun control laws and the citizenry was unarmed. This meant that there was no way to mobilize a second line of defense with a citizen militia. He was very afraid that if they did come across the channel, the gun control laws would probably be a major cause of the loss of England to the Third Reich.

A recent news story I heard that I seem to remember came out of Florida. It seems that there was a town down there that was having a serious crime problem. The mayor or city council, I do not remember the specifics, decided to require all citizens in the town to carry guns. Women were even told that when walking back to their cars from the stores to carry the gun in their hand so that it could be seen. With these rules in effect, the city did not have an increase in crime from the guns. In fact, the crime rate in the city dropped considerably.

Something I find interesting about this is that the media made what I would call an, "Oh, by the way" news story out of this. There was no serious discussion or analysis of this story. On the other hand, if there is a murder or a crime spree, the reporters are all over the story asking who did it and wanting to know why and how it was done. They ask the victims and their families what they thought about it or how the death of their loved one made them feel. Is it that the media needs crime to give them something to report? Why were they not all over that town asking people how they felt about the reduction in crime and having safer streets?

If there is no appreciable reduction in crime due to gun control and there are those who want to take advantage of the lack of guns, is it really a good idea? Or is it just a way to take the defenses away from the people so that the government has less resistance to doing whatever they want? Does this not make it easier for a tyrant to take control of the police and army and impose his control with having to worry about the citizens being able to oppose him? As I said, the government should be afraid of the people, not the people afraid of the government.

In some countries, all able-bodied people between roughly eighteen and the mid-forties are considered to be part of the army. These people are required to have automatic weapons in their homes to be ready to protect the country if they are needed.

From what I can find, these countries do not have any more or less gun crime than other countries. But at least the average citizens do have some way to defend themselves should anything happen.

Why is it that we are so focused on the gun and not other weapons? There are many other things that can be considered and are used as weapons. These items are also just as capable of causing injury and death. In fact, there are many more injuries and deaths caused by other items than are caused by guns.

Cars, for example, cause many injuries and deaths each year. Why are cars not classified as a weapon? Yes, many of these deaths and injuries are caused by accidents involving cars. There are also many cases where people used their car to deliberately injure or kill someone.

Baseball bats are well-known for being used in sports, but how many people have been severely beaten or even beaten to death with a baseball bat? I frequently hear of women being abused and beaten with baseball bats. Why isn't a baseball bat considered a weapon? Target shooting with a gun is considered a sport in the same way that baseball bats are used for sports.

People have also been beaten and killed with golf clubs. Yet this again is not considered a weapon like a gun.

A gun, a baseball bat, a car, and a golf club are all inanimate objects and none of them, in and of itself, is capable of injuring or killing someone. All of these items require a human to turn them into a deadly weapon. Saying a gun kills people is to ignore the fact that it is people who kill people. It does not matter what article is used to injure or kill people. If people want to injure or kill people, they will find something to use to do it with.

As seen by a recent death during a radio challenge, something as simple as drinking water can be used to kill someone. In the challenge, people were to see who could drink several gallons of water in the shortest period of time to win a prize. One woman wanted to get the prize for her children. She pushed herself to try to win the prize but instead she lost her life because of water poisoning. Almost anything can be used as a deadly weapon.

# *Patriot Act*

The Patriot Act was passed somewhat as a knee-jerk reaction to the events of 9/11. The government felt frustrated by the rules of law that limited their authority and ability to pursue terrorists by any means they felt they should be able to use. The intention was to be able to pursue terrorists and protect the country.

Similar to the tactics used by Hitler in Germany, they used the fears bordering on panic to get backing for the laws they wanted to get passed. They kept telling the people they would be overrun by terrorists if the laws were not passed.

This law overrides or bypasses many laws that are already established, even including some of the rights given in the Constitution. This law has the effect of minimizing or eliminating people's rights. This can be seen by some of the recent court decisions that have ruled some of the things being done under this act as unconstitutional.

When you pass laws limiting or eliminating people's rights, even for what is perceived as a necessity, you open the door to abuse and corruption. One of the biggest rights the law seems to ignore is the fact that we are supposed to be innocent until proven guilty. The fact that they can listen to our calls or hold us without going through the courts to establish probable guilt before they take action means that guilt is presumed.

I am sure we are never going to hear about all the problems this law has caused. I have heard the FBI has been found to be using the threat of being charged under this law to gather information without going through proper channels.

Millions of people travel in this country every day. A lot of them travel on commercial carriers. Because the terrorists used airplanes to commit their terrible acts on 9/11, the first thrust of taking our freedoms was against those who fly. (Does this mean we have put airplanes in the same category as guns?) These passengers became the first to feel the heavy hand of assumed guilt until proven innocent. Little old ladies with their knitting needles were presumed to be terrorists, and knitting needles were presumed to be their weapon of choice. Mothers with infants were presumed to be terrorists and were presumed to be hiding explosive materials in milk bottles. Men were considered to be terrorists, and their weapon was the pocketknife or nail clipper that they had carried for years.

I personally have carried a pocketknife for over fifty years, and in all that time, I have never used it as a weapon against anyone. Why does the government think that after fifty years of carrying a pocketknife I am now a terrorist and am about to use my knife to commit a terrorist act? My pocketknife has become such a dangerous terrorist weapon that even when I go to the Social Security office, I must take it back out to the car because they know I will be guilty of using it against someone there.

If we look at the number of people who traveled before 9/11 and those who have traveled since, these hundreds of millions of trips went normally and without many incidents. The percentage of incidents caused by travelers compared to the number of trips would be extremely small. There would probably be many zeroes after the decimal point before there would be a non-zero digit.

Also, look at all the stuff they have taken away from travelers since 9/11 and then think about how often these same items were carried before 9/11 without causing any problems. So, if these items were carried so often before without incident, why are they and those who carry them now considered to be terrorists? Why are the millions of average people and the average things they carry assumed to be guilty of terrorism without any proof they are an actual threat?

Why must we give up our rights and freedoms just because the government decided we are all guilty of being terrorists without any burden of proof of our being a threat? The more we allow the government to make decisions as to who is guilty without any due process, the more the government will be in control of our individual rights and freedoms. If we keep giving these freedoms away every time the government decides they need to control us, we will end up having no rights or freedoms left.

We all have things we use and carry every day. These are common items that in and of themselves are not dangerous. These are just things that we use every day to make our lives easier and/or more enjoyable.

If we look at all the things we have, I am sure there are people out there who could find some way to use them as a weapon to do harm to someone else. In most jails, many of these items are taken away because they could be used as weapons. Even bed sheets can be used to kill someone.

Now let's consider the Patriot Act and the rules being applied to travel and other things. Many common items are being banned in the name of security. This can be seen by the number of items that have been shown on television being taken away from airline passengers.

Does this mean we are not being considered any different than the prisoners in our jails? Have we given the government the power over us that the guards in the prisons have over their prisoners?

We need to think about how by allowing the government to use these and other laws to interfere with our rights to these common items, we are allowing them to in essence make and treat us as prisoners in our own country.

They say they are doing this to make us more secure from outside terrorists. My question then becomes who or what laws are protecting us from our own government?

Just like the terrorists in Iraq are making those people prisoners in their own country, is not our government making us prisoners in ours?

# Recent News and Reactions

In recent weeks there have been several news stories that have invoked many public responses and outcries. Many of these have been media-hyped, knee-jerk reactions calling for more governmental control or public outcries of indignation over the handling of the problem.

These reactions tend to bypass legal or procedural remedies for the problem or perceived wrong. In other words, these reactions are appealing to mob mentality that they must rise up against the injustice.

In the past year, the Mexican American community has held several marches for immigrant rights. The first march I saw in Phoenix and other areas had thousands of participants marching and carrying Mexican flags. This was quite an impressive sight.

These people were marching to get the immigration laws changed and many of them wanted a way to become U.S. citizens. This all goes to something I have discussed earlier, "What team do you play for?"

These people put a lot of effort into this march and were hoping to make a difference. The fact that such a large percentage of the participants were out there waving Mexican flags and only a few were waving American flags sent the strong message that they really did not want to be Americans. All they wanted was the benefits of being citizens without being responsible Americans. They wanted to be Mexican and remain Mexican because that was more important than joining the great melting pot that is America.

It appears that many leaders and members of the Mexican community who have been here for a long time also saw this. They realized that if they wanted to be accepted in the American society, they had to put America before their Mexican heritage.

This is not to say that their Mexican heritage is not important. As with the other ethnic groups, their ethnic heritage is important to them and the country. It is diversity of heritage that has helped build this great country.

There was a second march later on that summer. In this march, there were hundreds of American flags, and I did not notice more than one or two Mexican flags in the throng of many thousands of people. The leaders realized if they wanted to be accepted into the American melting pot, they had to show that they were more interested in being Americans of Mexican heritage than being Mexican Americans.

They had learned they needed to decide which team they wanted to play for.

In the past year since the first march, I have heard that the Mexican American community has started doing more things to join the American society like getting tax IDs so that they can file taxes without having a Social Security number.

They discovered something I have been saying. If you do not decide you want to play for the main team, you will have great difficulty in becoming a full member of that team.

Another news story is that Mr. Imus made some disparaging remarks about the Rutgers women's basketball team. Mr. Imus is a white man, and the members of the team are predominantly black. The words he used are predominant in rap music but are very disparaging to black women. Actually, the words would be disparaging to any women.

The immediate outcry from some of the supposed leaders in the black community reminded me of stories of a group that was very strong in the South many years ago.

At the risk of being politically incorrect, I am including the text of an e-mail I sent to a major cable news network when I started hearing the tone and direction of these leaders' comments.

> I see that the men in the black robes and black hoods have succeeded in surpassing the men in the white robes and white hoods. Not only do they have a larger following, but that following is all over the country as opposed to the more localized area of the men in white.
>
> These two groups are quite similar in many ways. I think that if you take the recent statements of the men in the black robes and black hoods and replace any references to blacks and replace them with similar references to whites and take any references to non blacks or others and replace them with similar references to blacks, the statements would sound very similar to those made by the men in the white robes and white hoods.
>
> Now the precipitating action to this recent outburst was a white man using common language of the blacks to make disparaging remarks about a predominantly black women's basketball team.
>
> Now I agree that these remarks were in bad taste and even crossed the line into slander and defamation of character. I also think this team and its school had good cause to take their case to court and sue for reparation.
>
> But the leaders of men in the black hoods did not seem to feel that this was good enough or the right approach. So instead they decided to incite their followers and other supporters into a frenzy. They were also able to get the media

involved by having them focus on how vile and hateful these remarks were. While their followers were in this frenzy, they were able to get them to kill a man's career and deny him his livelihood.

Things really haven't changed that much in the past couple of hundred years. The only thing that seems to have changed is the color of the hoods and robes.

I was very pleased with the coach of the basketball team's reaction to the incident. She was able to stay on the high ground and, while far from pleased with what had happened, she sought to handle the problem through more sensible and controlled means. She waited until she and her team had a face-to-face meeting with Mr. Imus to hear his side and his apology. They did not seek or desire mob justice but wanted only appropriate actions commensurate to the gravity of what actually transpired. She did not desire the loss of a man's livelihood for an unfortunate, off-the-cuff use of words.

Other members of the black community also felt the reactions of these supposed leaders of the black community were quite extreme and inappropriate.

I had a similar reaction during the aftermath of hurricane Katrina in New Orleans. Many of these same leaders came out with statements about how the government was using this catastrophe to suppress blacks. At that time it was my feeling that the people who were suffering the most were American poor. These were people of all races and creeds.

Back to the point—these inappropriate outbursts of by supposed leaders of the black community, or any group, tend to gain media attention. While these stories are sensational and generate ratings, the media again failed to do any questioning of the appropriateness of what was being said. By not questioning this, they were also responsible for loss of a man's job. They did put on many others from the black community who felt that the initial reactions were excessive. This was only done after the damage was caused.

By allowing groups to take the bully pulpit to push their agenda without question, we are not seeing the negative aspects of what is being said. We are allowing them to focus the attention through their colored glasses and toilet paper tubes.

Another tragedy that has occurred is the senseless killing of thirty-two people on the campus of Virginia Tech. This was a great tragedy that in many ways was blown out of proportion.

This would have been none the less a tragedy if it had stopped at the killing of the first two people. But it would not have attracted the amount of media attention and the subsequent mass knee-jerk reaction.

The media is so inundated with murders of one or two people, even in the college environment, that this would not have been as newsworthy. Because of the number of people who were killed in the incident, it generated a media frenzy.

When we have such a media frenzy, people tend to get extremely excited about the incident. Their excitement then translates into the need or desire to do something about the causes of the incident.

This excitement causes them to stop thinking rationally, and they tend to overreact and look for solutions that many people would normally consider extreme.

One interview I heard was with a swat team member at the site. He was saying he felt there should be more security on this and other college campuses. His ideas were to put keycard readers on all doors. He also wanted to station security guards at all doors to search all persons and bags going into every building.

While this swat team member was saying this, several students were interviewed and told what he had said. These students all disagreed with this approach and said that they liked their freedom and did not want to live in a police state.

I was very pleased and surprised to hear these students talk about the idea of a police state. I am impressed with the fact that these young people understood the difference between security and a police state. Politicians who are complaining about how the younger generation is tuning out should start realizing young people may have a better understanding of what is going on than politicians think.

Another recent local story was of a school board that had decided that once the high school students arrive on campus, they were not to leave the campus until the end of the school day. They were not allowed to go off campus to have lunch or run errands. I presume this board feels that high school students do not have any rights and that their desires or those responsibilities that their parents have granted them have no place in education.

Again, I was very pleased to see that these students along with their parents and their parents' permission took their protest to the streets. I personally do not think high schools should be run as prisons or just a place to keep kids during the school day.

It was also interesting to hear a representative of the school district say that this protest should have been held in the auditorium on the school campus. This would not have drawn the attention of the media and therefore the school board's attempts to lock up the students would not have drawn the attention to their efforts of absolute control.

This idea of extreme security has grown out of the 9/11 incident and the subsequent passage of the Patriot Act. This act is very similar to the Nuremberg laws of Germany. It gives the government extreme powers over the average people. It creates a police state similar to that of Hitler's Germany. It bypasses our constitutional rights to be assumed innocent until proven guilty. You are assumed to be guilty of carrying weapons you will use to harm others before you even get on a plane. I am sure all those little old ladies taking their knitting onto a plane are planning to use their knitting needles to take over the plane.

Another recent story is that California is moving up the date of its primary election. Is it in the best interest of the country for California to move its primary election to create a super primary Tuesday? Consider the fact that candidates must now be able to finance their campaigns in several states at the same time. California is a big state with big money. The need for large amounts of money to run campaigns in several large states means that candidates may now be forced to sell their souls to get the money.

Primaries are where relatively unknown people can try to make a run at the presidency or try to influence the platform others are running on. To do this in large states or multiple state primaries will take more money than these minor candidates would be able to raise. This almost guarantees that only major and/or well-known candidates will be able to afford to participate. Even then this may require them to sell out to large politically motivated groups seeking their own agendas. Having a long series of primary elections starting from the smaller states and progressively moving toward the larger states would give more candidates a chance to be heard.

Starting in a small state would mean that many candidates would have the opportunity to participate without having to have a large campaign fund. This would also give the candidate a chance to be seen and heard. If people like what they see and hear, they would be able to decide if they wanted to contribute to the candidate's campaign fund.

This would give the lesser-known (and possibly better) candidates the ability to start out small and still have a chance to build a larger organization, possibly going all the way. If they had to fight it out in the bigger or multi-state primaries early on, they would not have a chance against a well-funded or party favorite.

This means that voters would only have the major party-supported candidates to choose from, which in many cases leaves no real choice for many voters.

If California's purpose was to push out the minor candidates so that only those candidates from the large political organizations they support have a chance, they have succeeded.

Recently California has wanted the people of Arizona to build and pay for a power distribution line from their nuclear power plant to Palm Springs. California has always tried to be the leader on the social front. Here again they want to show they are the leader in limiting what they consider dirty industries. For many years they have tried to limit the building of power plants or oil refineries and the like.

To keep from having to build power plants, they want the people of Arizona to pay for a large power line from near Phoenix to Palm Springs so they can tap into the power from the nuclear plant the people of Arizona have paid for.

After this power line is built (if it is actually built), I am sure California will want to have a contract for power that states they will have first dibs on power during peak demands so their lights do not go out but causing the lights in Arizona to be dimmed for their benefit.

It seems that politicians do not want any dirty industries in California but are more than willing to have them in other states and to take advantage of them. This is another way for politicians to say they are strong environmentalists and also say they are better than other states even though they are asking those states to produce products they do not want produced in California.

Recently people and politicians are jumping all over the handling of the Iraq and Afghanistan war. There a lot of people who think we should just cut and run.

I find it interesting that many politicians have jumped on the bandwagon for political gain. Many, if not all, were among those who were originally in favor of the war and subsequently voted for it. These are leaders of the country who are supposed to be watching out for the country. These leaders are now caving to the pressure of the masses, and in order to save face, they are saying they were duped. How could so many of these people we trust be duped?

Another thing I find interesting is that many of those who now think they know how best to run or end the war are the same people who thought that they could solve the problem of the poor in the country. There are now more poor people in the country than there were, and their plight is getting worse or hopeless. As I have written elsewhere, they set out on that project without having an end game to get the people off of public support. Now they are saying they know what the end game should be for the war.

I am not saying the war is right or wrong. I am not going to discuss the reasons we went to war. These things are not important at this time. The thing that is important is the fact that we are now at war. We have told a country that we are there to help them get out from under a dictator. One thing the world had come to expect from America is that it was good to its word. If we told someone we were going to help them, we did it. We took over a failed attempt at building the Panama Canal, and we did it. We entered World War II to rid many occupied countries of the oppressive occupations that they were put under, and we did it. Both of these and others took sacrifice, but we were true to our word.

Now that we are engaged in the war, we must quit giving solace to our enemies by our political infighting. We all need to resolve to work to bring about a successful conclusion to the war. We need to let the world know that America is still a country of its word. We must not let all those average people in the war zones down by saying, "We came to help you, but oh well." If our government is not true to its word to other people in the world, how can we expect it be true to its own people? How can we trust politicians who do not think they should be responsible for the commitments of our government?

Something else I find interesting is the fact that in the early days of this country up through the Second World War, we were able to rally behind our government and the troops and win these wars. It is interesting to consider that as the government and the politicians have become more intrusive and controlling of the people, the people's support of the government and its ideas has decreased. It is interesting to consider that along with the decline in support of the government, the people have also lost interest in supporting its wars. This could explain the decline in the successes we have had in pursuing any war or police actions the government has engaged in.

The government-required testing of students has been a hot topic recently in my area of the country. The politicians and everyone else seem to be pleased that the scores on these tests have been going up for the past several years. These tests check reading, writing, and math. What I would be interested in knowing is with these scores going up, can or have the students read the documents such as: Thomas Paine's Common Sense, the Declaration of Independence, the Bill of Rights, and the other amendments. I would also like to know if they can they write an intelligent discussion on what they were about and what they meant in addition to just reading them?

I do not think parents or politicians even understand what these documents truly mean or what the ideas behind them were. A good case for this is the current condition of the country and our political scene. After all, these documents are the basic reason we have many of the rights we have. These are the basic documents that explain what is expected to live in this country. Or shall we continue to ignore building the foundation because we prefer to be more involved in trying to decorate the penthouse than worrying about the structure crumbling around us?

The tests also show that students now can do a better job in math. They know how to manipulate numbers better than before. They probably know how to calculate simple interest. My question is, do they really understand how interest works when it comes to their money? Do they really understand the long-term effects of these principles when it comes to their money? Have they been taught what compound interest can do to their debts or how quickly this interest can cause their finances to become a shambles?

Again, I do not think most of their parents or the politicians understand these things. This can be demonstrated by the number of people who have put themselves in such a financial bind because of not understanding what happens that they are either on the verge of bankruptcy or have filed for bankruptcy.

Why, then, are the numbers of people being caught up in financial scams and exorbitant interest loans growing even as these test scores are improving? Does this mean those who are designing these tests, which are supposed to show how prepared the students are for further education and life, themselves have not or are not prepared to understand the basic necessities to living in our current society?

The I-35 bridge collapse in Minnesota is another example of how Congress is falling down on their job to maintain the infrastructure of this great country. The Constitution states that the Congress shall have the power "to establish post offices and post roads." This means that they are responsible for the major roads in this country.

This is similar to politicians' work on helping the poor. They establish programs to start helping people and after getting them started, they fail to fund them sufficiently to actually accomplish their vision.

If I were to own a building with railings to keep people from falling off a balcony and the railing were to give way, I would be held liable. If it were found that I was aware of deterioration and did not repair it, I could be charged as being criminally negligent. Possibly I could be charged with criminally negligent homicide. Of course Congress will never be charged for this. Are they less equal than I am?

I find it interesting that Congress is more interested in paying for jet engines the military does not want or building ships that the navy does not want. They are interested in putting in off ramps on freeways to increase the value of their property or building bridges to nowhere they won't even maintain.

The politicians seem more interested in starting things or getting their pet projects slipped into bills than worrying about taking care of things they have started. They do not seem to be interested in really helping poor people or maintaining the infrastructure of the country or even funding education for all the people.

Another interesting fact is that politicians are now using this to blame the other party for the problem. And of course they have spent the taxes collected, so they want to raise gasoline taxes to pay for repairs to this and other bridges.

If they were putting up sports arena, they would not be talking about just taxing the arena but would also be talking about all the other tax revenue the project would generate. Why do they think major highways do not generate revenue from other sources? It is this infrastructure that gives people more opportunity to find other places to shop and work. People can find better paying jobs, better prices for products, and the ability to find and get to other things they would not be able to get to without the infrastructure.

All of this generates other tax revenue besides fuel tax. And as I discuss elsewhere, this kind of tax especially impacts the poor and the division between the haves and have-nots.

Recent news reports indicate that many politicians are calling for benchmarks for he progress in Iraq. It seems interesting that they do not have the same for things here in the United States.

There are many benchmarks that should be set here in the United States. Here is a list of possible benchmarks that should be placed on our government.

A benchmark for the repair and maintenance of bridges and roads. The Constitution calls for the maintenance of postal roads; therefore, the Congress is charged with this task.

A benchmark for the rebuilding of New Orleans.

A benchmark for being able to respond to a disaster.

A benchmark for the maintenance of dykes and sea walls. Many people are under the threat of disaster because of potential failure of these.

A benchmark for financing of schools and education. This can reduce the cost of helping people out of poverty and also reduce the number of people in our jails.

A benchmark for reducing the amount of "pork" that is added to spending bills.

A benchmark for following the Constitution and its intent.

A benchmark for protecting people's rights instead of taking rights away from the people.

A benchmark for having an end game for helping the poor and some way to get them off of public assistance.

A benchmark for stopping undue influence by large contributors.

A benchmark for stopping the socialization of the United States. This is giving preferential treatment for some groups at the expense of others. The Constitution is supposed to give us all equal rights.

A benchmark to stop bureaucrats and other political entities from having absolute power over the people they serve, such as giving them power to make rules and laws without the vote of the people.

A benchmark requiring full disclosure of the pros and cons of any plan or bill they want to pass.

# *Bullying*

In talking to many people, I get the feeling they are all feeling life has become more hectic and less enjoyable. They feel they do not have control over their lives and how they want to live it. Younger people ask if life were not simpler when I was younger. As I think about this, I have to agree that life seemed to be simpler when I was younger.

What is the difference between now and then? The more I think about it, the more I realize that the biggest change is that the number of people telling me how to live my life has grown. I realize that we have less control over how we choose to live our lives.

We have the government telling me that I can no longer carry my pocket knife onto an airline or into a government building even though I have done this for over years. We have organizations bullying the government into saying that I can not smoke in public areas even though people have been doing this for hundreds of years. We have governments bullying us into believing we are guilty until proven innocent even though the law of the land says we are innocent until proven guilty. We have governments bullying us into believing it is better to legislate than to educate.

We are being bullied into believing it is in our best interest that we should not be treated any better than those in jails. We are being bullied into believing many of the common items that we use every day are weapons, and we should not be allowed to carry them in public places. We are being bullied into believing that only the government knows what is best for us.

What do I mean by bullying's effect on society? After all, we are not a country of bullies, or are we? What is bullying? Bullying is where one person or group is doing something that another person or group does not like or feels that they can get an advantage by making an issue of it.

These are things like cultural differences, different ideas about how things should be done, and differences in lifestyles.

Bullying can be seen in things such as politicians or police setting low speed limits where most of the people are driving faster. Then to bully the people into compliance, we have the police out enforcing the imposed limit. We do this because we cannot or do not take the time to educate the people to travel at the speed we want. Also, politicians have found that by enforcing these low speed limits, they can raise more money.

Bullying is forcing people to use seat belts instead of educating them on the advantages of using them. This is also a method for insurance companies to bully the people into doing something that is to the insurance companies' advantage.

Is our adult life any different than it was when we were in school? When most of us were in school, we all had to deal with bullies of one form or another. There always seemed to be someone who did not like us for some reason or another. Many of these people always seemed ready and willing to make an issue of things in front of other people to make themselves look better.

It might be interesting to look at the environment that many of the bullies or controlling people grew up in.

When children are very young, they need to be in a very controlling environment. They need strong guidance so that they learn that that red burner on the stove is a danger or that they should not run out into the street. They need this strong control because they have not yet developed the understanding or the cognitive ability to realize what is dangerous and what is not.

As these children get a little older and start to understand some of the dangers, we need to slowly back away from these controls and start working on other controls that are appropriate for their new age. We need to teach them how to ride a bicycle, play baseball or soccer, and how to get along with their friends. We need to teach them how to study and how to learn from their environment and from other people. We also need to understand that they are starting to become individual people and start accepting that they have some of their own ideas. We need to encourage them to think about what they are doing and help them understand how their ideas fit into the world. We must encourage their good ideas and traits and try to show them the problems with their bad ideas and traits.

We must remember that from infancy to young adulthood and finally to adulthood, their minds and bodies are continually changing. Just as they are changing, we must also change our approach to parenting. We must start out with some strict rules, changing to more of a guiding approach. Finally, when they are an adult, we must step back and let the training we have provided be the controlling factor in their lives.

Unfortunately, in a large number of homes and families, the child grows both mentally and physically but those rearing them do not. They tend to stay with an approach that was appropriate for a younger age. The child or young adult's mind is developing a greater understanding of life and the world, but their discipline and guidance does not reflect this. This discrepancy starts to lead to confusion and possibly rebellion in some form. The child will look for other ways to start exercising control of his environment that is within his level of understanding. Depending on their age and comprehension, some will turn to food, some will start acting out in school, and if the control at home is severe enough, they will start looking for others to bully.

I guess what I am trying to say is that the need to control or bully other people is in many cases a by-product of how we bring up our children. If we do not allow our parenting methods to grow with our children, we start to teach them that control or bullying is an appropriate behavior. They will then take these lessons and apply them to their actions in later life.

Some time ago Oprah did a show that focused on bullying in schools. They showed a program that would take a freshman class and put them in an auditorium. They would then ask those who felt they were bullied or demeaned in some particular manner to step to the other side of the room. They would then talk to them about how the bullying made them feel and how they felt toward those who had made them feel that way. They would then ask for any of those who performed these acts to speak up and talk about why they did this and how the responses made them feel. This process was repeated over and over with different types of bullying or demeaning.

By the end of the day, almost everyone, including some teachers, ended up on one side of the room or the other. It also appeared that bullying by one group against others led to bullying of others by those being bullied. This would indicate that bullying or demeaning leads to more bullying and demeaning, and thus the problem is self-feeding.

There was a lot of soul searching by many of the people who went through the program. The result was that many of the problems the administration had been dealing with in the school disappeared.

This type of bullying and demeaning was related to the actions that were going on in the Columbine High School that led to one of the worst school shootings in the country. The students who did the shooting had been bullied and demeaned because they were different and the jocks did not like the way they were. The more popular kids pushed them to the breaking point, and they felt they had no other way to stop it.

Now let's take a look at the general society. We are seeing more and more where one group has decided their idea of what people should do or how they should act is being put into laws. These laws are in effect a form of bullying by one group against another group whom they feel is not as good as they are.

One of the results of this is that other groups are feeling the only way they can protect themselves and their likes is to work to pass laws that protect or enforce rules they want or feel are right. As these rules and laws are enforced, other groups are deciding the only way they can defend themselves is to do the same and work to get their ideas made into laws. As one can see, this is an activity that becomes self-feeding and ever increasing.

Another result is that those who feel they do not have the power to fight this or get their ideas put into law look for other ways to get what they want. Some of them just drop out. Others turn to drugs. Others turn to other illegal activities. Some even turn to pure violence as a way to strike back at those they feel are using the system to bully them.

All of these activities again result in other groups trying even harder to control these people and their activities. They do this saying it is for the common good that we must put more control on these people.

Where does this spiral end? When do we figure out that the more we try to control others behaviors, the more they try to control us or the more we drive people to violence against everyone?

As we have seen, bullying is a problem in our schools starting in grade school and escalating into high school. But does it really end there? As we move beyond school, we start getting into the larger world. We now start finding power in political activism and politics itself. Starting with homeowners' associations and small-town politics, we start finding the power to push our ideas of how things should be done. We find that using education to get our ideas accepted is either too slow or does not completely get the results we want. We soon discover that by passing laws, we can say this is the way it must be done.

We find that trying to get other people to push and support the laws and rules we want is difficult. We learn that the best way to get the laws we want is to run for an office in the government. The best way to do this is to find rules the constituency wants to impose on others. We talk to different groups about how we are going to help them get their rules enforced. This is not unlike the popular jock in school who, in order to increase his popularity, gets involved with other people and their bullying. Now that we have become popular enough and are elected, we find that we only have to convince a few other people to get our rules passed. This is much easier than having to convince a larger group. We work within this smaller group and help them push their ideas on the people so they will help us push our ideas.

If while we are trying to get our ideas put forth, we find there are people or groups in our political arena who do not agree with our ideas, we find ways to get around them. We find others in the group with whom we can make alliances to either marginalize or bully those opposed into supporting their ideas. This bullying is done by getting enough support to make sure any ideas put forth by the opposition are not implemented.

If we are successful in bullying our ideas here, we may decide that our ideas of what people should do and how they should act is bigger than the local political scene. We may decide to take our ideas that we need to bully people into doing things our way to a larger stage. To do this we must move on to county, state, and federal politics.

All the time we must remember that to get the votes, we must depend on those who also think their ideas are the right way to go. We must depend on the fact that they feel pushing or bullying their ideas into laws will make them feel more in control or powerful. We need to help feed their bullying to get them to help us do the things we want to do, much like in high school, we must feed and support other people's bullying to get them to feed into and support our bullying.

You may think I am dwelling on bullying in politics too much. But I do not think that it is by accident that the platform given to those in power is often called "the bully pulpit."

Another tool politicians have found to press their ideas and thus bully the people is electronics. They have found they can put up photo radar and photo red light cameras to help them impose their will and force people to do things their way. They do not want to think about the fact that there may be better ways to set up the red lights or that their speed limits may not be appropriate. They feel the way they have decided to establish these things is right just because they have the power, and they are always right. To prove they are right, they will then start bragging about how many people they have bullied by issuing tickets for something they may have set up wrong. They are also bullying the people into thinking they are right in thinking people are guilty until proven innocent. Since there is no way of calling the cameras into the court to question them on the circumstances, politicians now have a form of absolute power over the people.

Just think of what Hitler could have done in Germany if he had the tools that are now available to our politicians—the ability to use photo enforcement of laws; the ability to electronically eavesdrop on our conversations and phone calls without our even knowing it; the ability to look at our purchases on credit cards or store cards; the ability to call us in because we said something out of context or made purchases that may be similar to those that would be made by a terrorist; the ability to put us into a database as someone of interest because during our normal activities we did or said something that some bully in the government thought could be a threat.

With all this bullying to get us to do or act as some politician thinks we should, it is not a stretch to see why people today feel life is more stressful than it was in the past.

The media is another group that has "the bully pulpit." They have the ability to put forth their ideas to large numbers of people at one time.

To get the ratings the media needs to attract advertisers, they must find ways to get people to pay attention to them. To get people to pay attention, they must find ways to get people to feel they are on their side.

One way is again to make people feel they are one of them. They try to make people think they have some of the same feelings the media has. They, like the bullies in school, want to try to show they are better by making other people feel or appear smaller.

With the growing feeling that people have no control over their lives, it becomes easier for the media to get their attention by showing other people's problems.

In high school when someone was sent to the principal's office, the bullies would start hooting and hollering about it in front of their friends to get attention. The media is calling attention to people who have had a problem with the law and have paid their debt to society. Is this any different than the bully in school who wanted to make themselves feel superior and attract the attention of their friends?

Another way the media supports bullying is by supporting and giving the use of the bully pulpit to those who wish to control our lives. They support the idea that we are guilty until proven innocent without questioning the basis or reasoning behind this concept. They are willing to focus on small numbers and percentages, showing how bad something is, to get the people interested in what they are saying. They do not seem willing to show the effect on the larger numbers of people who will be affected by the action they are supporting. They are willing to bully the people into believing that supporting the loss of freedoms of the larger number of people is in their best interest without pointing out the effect of this loss of freedoms mean.

With our media outlets supporting and even engaging in this bullying, again it is not a stretch to see why people today feel life is more stressful than it was in the past.

I know this seems counter to popular beliefs. How can I talk about religion and bullying?

Over the ages, religions have been at the forefront of education. They at many times have been the only source of education. This has always been a commendable pursuit and is very important to the development and improvement of societies.

With this in mind, where does bullying fit in? When you are educating, you are teaching people to think. When you teach people to think, you are giving people tools to deal with their lives. For me, the problem comes when you stop teaching and start legislating. This is when you stop teaching people how to live and start telling them they must live their lives by the rules established by religions.

If you look at most of the great religious writings, you can find many different views in each of them. These different views give you a broad view of life. They show that at any given time a different view may apply. These all give you a basis for being able to understand things that are happening.

When religious leaders dwell on a specific portion of these writings and use them to say that is how people should act, they are crossing over from educating to legislating. They are using those specific passages to bully their students into agreeing with their views without taking the broader view of the rest of the writings.

When these leaders take these writings and not only try to bully their followers into following these writings but also tell their followers they must bully others into following their ideas, they have fully converted from teachers to a true bully. They have perverted religion from a platform of teaching to a platform for bullying and control.

Many of those in religions are aware of this and are truly dedicated to teaching. I also do feel that if we look at what is going on in the world today, we can see where there are many that fall into the category of using religion for bullying and control.

With our religious leaders trying to bully everyone into living our lives the way they think they should be lived instead of educating them, it is not a stretch to see why people today feel life is more stressful than it was in the past.

There are many organizations, including nonprofits, for-profit, and true business organizations, that also have crossed over from seats of learning and education to bullying.

These are organizations were formed to study and find solutions to problems. They have become discontent with just educating or supplying solutions. They have decided their solutions are the only correct solutions and that they must bully the people and politicians into making their solutions into the law.

They are not satisfied with the speed that education provides for solving these problems. They are not concerned that there may be flaws in their solutions nor that someone else may also have a solution. They are only interested in seeing that their solution becomes the only solution. Like any good bully, they are not concerned by how other people feel about their ideas; they are only concerned by how they and their friends feel. They will use any means they can to convince enough people that their solution is right.

With this in mind, does this mean that even though 51 percent of the people agree with an idea, that it is no less bullying? With every group or organization that we come in contact with or deal with trying to bully us into doing things their way, does this not make our lives more stressful?

Whatever happened to the idea of education instead of legislation or bullying? If you cannot convince people that your ideas are the best through education, it may mean your ideas are not the best for everyone.

# Business and Industry

I talk a lot about politicians and other groups trying to control the citizens of the country. I think I should also talk about business and industry trying to control their customers.

We have businesses, such as those in the computer industry, that use many different methods to control their customers. One company has been known to work to get their people hired into companies so that they can get products placed into these companies.

There are also corporations that, when trying to replace another corporation's products for a company, will low-ball their estimates of cost. They convince these companies they can do the job cheaper and easier than their current vendors. They will get in and start converting to their products with enough material to get the project started and create enough investment that the company thinks they must continue the project. They then find they need a few more products to complete a certain portion of the project. Then when this is completed, they find other products are needed. By this time, they have the company so invested in the change that they cannot go back even though the project is now way over its original estimate. Unfortunately, these companies find out too late that the final cost is many times what the corporation had originally estimated.

There are software corporations that sell major software components such as operating systems. They get their customers on these systems. The customers then buy other software and hardware to use with these systems. After a few months or years, the corporation will completely re-write their system. They will then set a date they will stop supporting the older system. This forces the customers to upgrade to the newer version. One thing customers may find with the upgrade is that the other software and hardware they were using may no longer work, forcing them to spend more money to upgrade these as well.

I worked with software from a corporation that had the philosophy that their software was backward compatible. This meant that when you upgraded their software, your other software and hardware would still work. In fact, we had software that was over twenty-five years old and it still worked. Much of this software was business- or industry-specific and would have caused a major upheaval in the company to replace it. Needless to say, other corporations did everything possible to convince business that this type of software was a bad idea.

There are other corporations that make consumer products they sell in their own stores. There are many different corporations that make similar products, and in fact, some of their products are made by these other corporations. While their products are made by other corporations, they will have them change critical parts to their own design so that when the product breaks, the customer will have to go to their stores or repair services to get the parts. This can be a real problem for people who live way out in the country and are not close to the stores or repair services for the product.

Another interesting phenomenon that is pervasive in business and industry it the idea, "If it is not invented here, it has no merit." This not only applies to ideas that may come from outside the company, but it also applies to department managers who think they have the only answers. It applies to the VPs who do not consider the ideas of their managers. It applies to those in the boardrooms who think they are the only ones who know how things are to be done. It even applies to politicians who think they are the only ones who know what is best for the people.

Have you ever made a call to a customer service department and been put through to an automatic answering system that has a series of choices and your question does not really fit into any of the selections? This was probably put together by someone or some group who thinks they know what everyone wants and really does not care to think or hear there are other possibilities. Or you get a person who has some script they must go through that contains dozens of questions or suggestions that have no relevance to your problem or that you have already tried. If these people were more open to other ideas or to listen to their customers, they would probably make changes to their systems.

I personally have had many occasions where I tried to tell managers what they were trying to do would not produce the results they were looking for. They did not want to listen to what I had to say because it would mean they did not have sound ideas. Some of them would respond by saying that if it didn't work, I could come back and tell them "I told you so." Because it was not invented in their office, it was not a good idea, and on several occasions, I finally did go back and tell them "I told you so." I guess my frustration with being ignored so many times finally came through.

This reminds me of something that happened in a steel factory. I think this was somewhere in the south. The company was looking for ways to improve their processes and correspondingly their profits. They decided to offer a large bonus based on the amount of savings to *any* employee who turned in an idea that created an improvement. One of the line employees turned in a suggestion that was implemented. The president of the company stayed true to his word and personally presented the employee with his first bonus check. The president said he was a little choked up at the prospect but had to remember the savings to the company. The reason he was so choked up is that this line worker's check was bigger than his own was. Yes, the line worker made a lot of money for his idea, but the company profited even greater. This just goes to show that managers and engineers are not the only ones who have great ideas. Good ideas can be generated or invented anywhere and not just in paneled offices.

Another way to try to control people is the "store card." Businesses tell you that you can get a better price by using their store card. Since most all major stores have store cards and, as I have found, they do not carry all the products I need, you must have cards from many stores to get the benefit. For some people and people who travel, you may end up with hundreds of cards to carry to get the benefit.

One thing this means to the consumer is that if they do not have or carry a card for that store, they are going to get shafted on the price of products. If these businesses were to do away with their two-tier pricing structure and give the same price to everyone, we would all benefit. They could advertise lower prices on a product and everyone who wanted it could get the benefit.

Many years ago my family had a business and back then there was another attempt at an idea to get people to go to one store over another. There were companies that developed things like Green Stamps or Gold Bond Stamps and others. People received a stamp for each dime they spent. These stamps were then pasted in books and the books of stamps could be turned into their appropriate corporation to purchase products they had in their catalogs.

This idea grew and most all business were giving stamps of one type or another. People started ending up with many different types of stamp books and never getting enough of any type to get what they wanted. They soon grew tired of licking stamps and trying to figure out what to do with all the partial books of stamps they had. They stopped being interested in all the hassles, and these stamps stopped producing the results that they were touted to create. These stamp promotions eventually virtually disappeared.

I was very surprised when I went to a chain grocery in my area and found out they had discontinued their store card program. They said the customers and clerks were getting tired of the hassle of the cards and the corporation had decided it was not worth the trouble. While I was surprised they had discontinued their card, I was equally surprised they had instituted a stamp program you had to paste on a large sheet. When you filled the sheet, you would earn a special gift product (which I was not interested in getting anyway).

I am happy to see that at least some businesses are realizing that these cards are becoming more of a problem and nuisance than the benefit that they produce.

This, in many ways, is similar to other things I have discussed in this book—things such as HMOs, homeowners' associations, and the like. Like all of these things, the store card and stamp promotions have an initial appeal to certain groups of people. When others see the success that occurs with this group, they jump in and try to apply it to everyone. As more and more people get involved, you get more and more people who are not really into these types of tactics. As more of these people are pushed into these projects, there becomes more dislike and distrust of the idea and it ends up not being as good as it was expected to be when it started.

What has happened to customer service? In the past many companies learned that if they wanted to survive and succeed in their businesses, they had to take care of their customers. They learned they needed to listen to their customers so they could find better ways to service them. They learned they needed to provide a quality product and quality service.

Currently it seems that companies think listening to the customer is sending out customer surveys designed to give the companies the answers they want to hear. These surveys seem more designed to feed the marketing ego of the company than to find out what the customers are really thinking.

What I find interesting is that many of these large companies have a large staff of frontline customer service people interfacing with their customers every day. I am sure these people are hearing a lot of what the customers are feeling about the company. I wonder how many of the higher executives hear about the comments these people are getting from the customers. Do they have a structure in place to have both the good and bad comments sent up the chain of command unfiltered or are they categorized in very narrow groupings that tend to make the company look better? Another problem with this is that lower-level managers want to make things look better and tend only to pass along the good comments.

I know most, if not all, of the grocery chains have tried all sorts of things to try to get and hold customers. They have used stamp programs, store cards, prize programs, and others. Quite a number of years ago, my family did business with a large chain grocery store. This particular store was size-wise one of the smaller stores in the chain. But despite its smaller size, it was one of the busier and more profitable in the chain. In fact, the manager was eventually promoted because of the success of the store. A new manager was put in his place. Under this new manager, the store slowly started losing customers and not too long after that, I noticed that the space it occupied had become a shoe store.

What happened? Well, the old manager was willing to keep things in stock that people wanted. The people in the neighborhood knew they could go there and find what might be considered unusual food items they would occasionally use to vary their meals. Many of these items may not sell often, but they were things people knew they could find there if they wanted them. Because of this, people became loyal customers and did most of their shopping there.

When the new manager took over, I (and I assume many of the other customers) started to notice that many of these somewhat unusual products started disappearing from the shelves. As these items disappeared, the number of customers also started to decline.

I am sure this new manager was probably well trained in the company's policies and ideas on how to run a successful store. I know many companies and their bean counters have decided that inventory turns are more important than anything else. What this means is that it is more important that every square foot of shelf space be stocked with items that sell frequently than to have items that do not move that frequently. This means that the unusual items people may be trying to find have no place in their stores.

This means customers will have to find other stores to try to find the items they are looking for. Understanding this and trying to give customer service is probably why the first manager was so successful. He understood that if he had more of the products people were looking for, they would be more likely to do their shopping in his store. The bean counters are trying to compensate for this by putting a lot of what I would call junk items in their stores to get people to think they are taking care of them.

Another factor in customer service (or the lack thereof) is the instituting of store brands. Recently we went to a store to find a particular skin-care cream that had been the most successful for us. What we found was that the selection of national products had been greatly reduced and the particular product we were looking for was no longer on the shelves. What we did find is that the shelf space had been replaced with store-brand products. While many will say these products are made by the same companies as the national brands, no one is saying who is making it or if the formulation is the same as the brand we were looking for. This leads us to a problem; either we start trying to find out which store brand and from what store works as well as the product we were looking for or we stop buying from the store and buy what we want online. To start trying the various store brands presents another problem. Some of us have allergic reactions or rashes that occur from some product formulations. In fact, I know people who are allergic to whole product lines from some of the national brands. So this means we must try the various store brands with the probability that many of these products might cause rashes and the like. Does putting the customer in this position really show that the stores are interested in customer service? This all can be said for many of the store brands and the unknown problems that people will have while trying to find a suitable replacement for a known product they spent years finding.

Recently some family friends were on a trip to a wedding. These friends do not have a lot of money. They are struggling, like many other families, to keep their heads above water. Also, due to some problems in the past, they do not have great credit. They have been working hard to get their credit back in proper order and in the process have gotten rid of their credit card debt and credit cards.

Enough of background and on to the story. To take this trip, they had gotten some help from family members to buy a newer car, as their car was not that dependable. They were traveling on the interstate in a sparsely populated area when they had a problem with a wheel bearing and had to be pulled off the road. They then had to be towed a fair distance to a somewhat larger town. This cost them about two hundred dollars just to be towed. This problem occurred late on a Friday afternoon, and they could not get the car to a service station to be checked out that evening, so they and their three children were going to need a place to stay for at least that night.

Knowing their situation, I decided to try to help them through their emergency and worry about who was going to ultimately pay the bills later. First, I tried to get them a room in a motel and have it put on my credit card. I called the motel to try to make the reservation. They told me I could use my credit card to reserve the room, but they would need to have it there when they checked in. I would have been more than happy to do this except for the fact that I was over twelve hundred miles away from them. I was also over one hundred miles from the nearest major airport, and they were two to three hundred miles from the nearest major airport, which would make it impossible for me to get there in any reasonable time. As you can see, it would have been impossible for me to be able to present my credit card in person within any reasonable time.

Now as to customer service. This was a well-known major motel chain, but with the Internet, and even with them having motels in their chain that were very close to my home, there was no way that I could do anything to get them a room for that night. The motel had their strict corporate rules, and there was no way they could bend their rules, even to help someone in trouble.

My friends fortunately had enough money to get the room, but after paying for the towing and the room, they were going to be very short on money and not have much left to get food, let alone get the car fixed and pay for the nine hundred miles to get back home.

The next morning they were able to have the car looked at and it was determined that the necessary parts could not be shipped in until Monday morning. This meant they would be stranded in the town and not be able to make the wedding. I decided that being stranded in a small town with three kids, one who had just turned one year old, was not going to be pleasant for them. With this in mind, I found that there were two major rental car agencies in the town, so I started making calls to them to see if I could rent a car so my friends could to try to still get to the wedding or at least be able to drive to get food and entertain the kids. Again, I got the same response from the local car rental agencies. If I was not there to present a credit card and sign the forms, there was no way I could get them a car.

At this, I decided to try calling the corporate 800 number for one of the car rental agencies. I got through to a supervisor and he was not very sympathetic to the problem. He only told me that the corporate policy did not allow for any other way to get the car for them. They had to present a credit card in their name (which they did not have) or I had to be there to present my card and ID to be able to rent a car. There was no other way to do it.

I then tried the other rental car 800 number. I was able to get through to a supervisor with this company. This one also told me the same thing, but he at least tried to contact the local agency to see if there was any way they could help. Unfortunately, it was now after noon and that agency was closed. He then contacted an agency at a mid-sized airport about one hundred miles away. He tried to work with them to see if they could find some way to help, without any luck. At least this customer service supervisor tried to give customer service even though his hands were tied by corporate policy. I would like to again thank this customer service supervisor for Enterprise Rent-A-Car for his efforts in trying to give customer service in someone's time of need.

Needless to say, all my efforts to give these people some emergency relief from my home were thwarted by corporate rules and regulations that are definitely not geared toward customer service when someone is in need of customer service.

These people were forced to spend Friday night through Monday morning in the motel with their three children. I did wire these people some money so they would be able to get the car fixed, pay for the room and food, and have enough to get back home. I was not able to get them to the wedding or to get them transportation so they could at least be able to drive to get food or find things to keep the children entertained. They had to walk several miles in near one hundred-degree heat to do these things.

I would think these large corporations would want to be known for customer service, especially when someone has an emergency and someone else is trying to help them. Isn't this is what is meant by the words "customer service"? Isn't this a time when the customer is most in need of "customer service"? Should this not be the time when any large corporation could shine and show how committed they are to helping their customers? It is a perfect opportunity to show how compassionate they are by doing everything they can to help someone in need, especially when it is not going to cost them anything and in fact will help them to sell more of their services.

Another downside to store and credit cards, especially since 9/11, is the fact that they track your purchases. As I have seen on many of the police-type shows on television, the police are able to track people and the things they buy using their cards.

Since 9/11, we have had laws passed such as the Patriot Act and government agencies such as the FBI that have abused these laws to get information on people. With these types of activities going on, it is not a far stretch to think the government would gain access to this information. With their ability to get their hands on this information, it leaves open the possibility of abuse of the information.

This means that with this information, they are able to build profiles of people. This means that just because you buy certain types of cold medicines and certain other products, they can make an assumption that you are using them to make illegal drugs. If you have recently purchased a certain type of rope, you can become a suspect in a crime where that type of rope was used. If you purchased a certain unique type of shoe, you could become a person of interest in a crime where that type of shoe was worn.

If some of your purchases are similar to those that would be needed by a terrorist, the federal government could quickly get into your life to see what you are doing.

At the least all of these things could be done without your knowledge. This could lead to investigation and many types of interference in you life. This could also lead to unwarranted and irreparable damage to job, business, credit, or personal credibility. In other words, information could be abused and it could be used to ruin your life without reason.

We have many interstate businesses such as trains, planes, busses, as well as a large number of chain stores. Many of them, especially where transportation between states is involved, find it very difficult to keep up with the various rules. Every time they cross a state line, the rules change. If this presents problems to businesses, think about how much stress this can add to the average person.

This is a magnifying glass on what I see as a general problem through out the country. Yes, we are a country of laws, but how many laws are enough, and how many laws are too much? Are we to have a law every time some group decides they have a better idea? Do we really need to make laws to meet every situation?

Should we be making it as complex and frustrating to businesses and to the individual? What is happening to our individual and business rights?

It is extremely difficult for any person or entity to serve more than one master. The more we have individuals or groups developing different and sometimes opposing laws, the more impossible it becomes to please anyone, let alone not being in violation of someone's laws.

Is it any wonder that more and more people seem to be looking for some relief from the mayhem, and many are turning to drugs? Look at the increase in the usage of legal sedatives or relaxers, let alone illegal drugs.

Not unlike politicians, business and industry are another group that does everything they can to spin the numbers. They hire media consultants to help them put a favorable "spin" on some public relations problem they may have. They will hire advertising agencies to not only to put a good face on their products but to also try to hide any negative facts about the products.

An example is a TV advertisement that was on frequently about a year ago that I have not seen in recent times. This was an ad for some high-powered headlights for cars. They continually pressed the idea that the driver would be able to see the road better. They showed the driver coming around a curve and being able to see an animal in the road sooner. They also showed a child appearing in the road and said how much sooner the driver would be able to see him. They talked about how much safer it would be for the driver and for other things in the road. They never talked about coming around a curve on some dark, two-lane road and meeting another driver coming from the other direction. They never said anything about how much brighter these lights would be in the eyes of that driver. They did not talk about the possibility that the other driver might be partially blinded by the brighter lights or how this might cause that driver to drift over the centerline because he may not be able to see as well. I also find it interesting that a similar headlight was tried about ten years ago and it also disappeared.

Another interesting ad that was running recently concerns a solar-powered fan to help ventilate your parked car in the summertime. In this ad, they talk about how this item would make your car considerably cooler. They showed a closed car with a thermometer in it. They showed how hot this car got in the sun. They then reiterated how much this item would cool the car, but they never showed a similar car in a similar situation and what the temperature was in that car. This tells me that their cooler does not make a big enough change to make any significant change in temperature.

If someone were to take a critical look at the advertisements we see, they would find that many of them have some very significant problems that are not disclosed to the public.

It is interesting how businesses have used the courts to diminish the power of their competitors and gain an advantage.

One of the largest of these I can think of is the breakup of AT&T. Sprint and MCI were among the companies that were instrumental in the breakup. The whole thrust of the breakup was the cost of long-distance services. One thing that most people did not realize was that AT&T was using the higher long-distance rates to subsidize local telephone service. Their idea was that the kids could not call grandma if grandma couldn't afford to have a telephone. After the breakup, the cost of local phone service rose as the cost of long distance went down. Also, the results of the research at the AT&T laboratories became privileged and were not put out for everyone's advantage.

With the new technologies that have been developed that allowed more calls to be carried with less cost, more competitors entered the market. With this greater competition, the pressure on all the long-distance carriers increased. Some of those were even forced into bankruptcy.

Another problem that came out of the breakup was the number and complexities of billing became evident. People had to track and pay multiple bills. The various carriers were now charging for calls coming from another carrier. There were more hands in the process of billing and more taxes involved. It is also interesting that there is now a tax listed on the phone bills to help subsidized low-income families so they can have a phone. Isn't this what AT&T was doing in the first place and the reason they had higher long-distance charges? Hey, doesn't this give the politicians another opportunity to get their hands on money so they can help people and show that they care?

While the breakup may have made many of those involved rich, it is my opinion that the overall effect is that the people are paying more than necessary for a more confusing system because there is less cost but more hands are involved in the phone calls and their billing.

Many times in our short history the government has tried to use its heavy hand to control businesses. One example that comes to mind happened several years ago.

The people were becoming outraged at the cost of products and how fast they were rising. One main example was the price of cars. People felt these prices were rising too fast. To counter this, the government imposed a freeze on the price of cars shortly after the new model-year cars came out and their prices were established. This meant that the auto manufacturers were forced to maintain the same price for that model year.

In the following years, the auto manufacturers developed a new advertising scheme. They started giving factory rebates on their cars. That is, that they would give the customers back a large cash amount based on the price of the car. While this might seem like an interesting marketing idea, it actually served a very different purpose.

The automakers actually raised the sticker price of the cars roughly 10 percent above where they would normally have set them. This meant a couple of things. If the government decided to again try to freeze the prices of the automobiles, they could vary the amount of the rebates they would give. They then could be able to raise the prices even though they were frozen. Also, when the PT Cruiser came out, the automaker realized it had set the price too low for the demand. With the rebate method, it could in effect raise the price without changing the sticker prices just by changing the amount of rebate they offered.

While this may not be an example of what we might consider a business, it is a good illustration of the lack of respect big corporations or organizations have for their customers.

Several years ago, I went into the local office of the Red Cross and made, for me, a couple of fairly large donations. One was for tsunami relief and the other was for hurricane relief on the gulf coast.

I made these donations with one request. I requested that my name not be put on any mailing lists. Even with this request, I started receiving mail from them. At first I would just throw the letters away. As they continued to arrive, I started to become irritated, and I started keeping the mailings. Occasionally they did get discarded, but at the present time I have a file of about twenty-fie pieces of mail they have sent me.

I made those donations to try to help other people. My request to not have my name on their mailing list was for a couple of reasons. First, is that these mailings cost them money, and I wanted more of my money to go to those in need. Second, I do not like getting ads and solicitations in the mail. If I am going to donate to a cause, I do it because I want to, not because someone is hounding me to make a donation.

Also, it seems that my other junk mail has increased, and I wonder if they have sold my name to other mailing lists. This is like what happened during the great depression. Panhandlers would in some way try to put a chalk mark on those who gave them food or money. This was to let other panhandlers know that this person was one who would give them money. This is probably where the term "mark" originated. I am not pleased with the idea that any group is using me as a mark or letting anyone else know that I might be a good mark for them.

Needless to say, I have not made any more donations to the Red Cross.

I do give to other charities. One of them was the local food bank. I have made a couple of donations to them with the same request. I believe I have only received one piece of mail from them. This was a thank you for the donation. I have considered giving them other donations, but they are in the middle of the town, and with all the electronic traffic control and ticketing the town has installed, I avoid going into town. Sorry folks, but the city wants to supposedly reduce accidents, but in the process they have driven me and many of my friends to do business elsewhere.

# Government Medical Insurance

Everyone seems to think having the government take over medical insurance is going to be a cure-all for the medical insurance problems. There have been a lot of politicians, media types, and others who have been painting this idea as the greatest thing since sliced bread. They paint a picture of the government giving everyone all the medical services they will ever need. They will be able to get any procedure or medicine they need when and where they need it.

They tell people about all the problems people are now having with the current system and, without explaining how, leave the people with the idea that all these problems will be solved when the government takes over. They are very liberal with the discussions of these problems, yet they never talk about how a government-run plan will be any better.

Another thing they are talking about is the cost of health insurance. They keep pointing out how much health insurance costs, but they never talk about how much it will cost to have the government run the system. They also do not talk about how it will be funded.

One of the problems I see in medical care is that some doctors are great at treating the symptoms but fail to treat the underlying cause. They may treat a rash with a salve when the underlying cause is a failing internal organ that may be causing toxins to build up in the system, which in turn is causing the rash. How many times have you heard of people who got a second opinion that discovered the root cause of an ailment?

Many people are yelling about how they can cure the ills of the health-care system. They are setting themselves up as doctors who know what the root problem is and how they can solve it. My question is, are they just trying to treat the symptoms or are they looking at the root cause of the problem? Are they just looking at the fact that the costs of medical care have been going up or are they looking at *all* the hidden costs that are causing that problem?

I remember an instance when I was traveling with my family. My son had allergies and occasionally would have to go to the doctor to get an allergy shot. We had traveled from California to central Illinois. The doctor had given us his medicine to take with us in case he needed a shot, with the stipulation that we have a doctor check him and administer the shot. We went to the local doctor to have him checked, and he gave my son the shot. When it came time for me to pay the bill, I was expecting to pay the usual fee plus a little extra for a first-time visit. This, I was expecting, would be in the range of fifty to seventy-five dollars or more. I was very surprised when the doctor charged me twelve dollars for the visit. What is it that made a basic doctor visit worth fifty dollars in California and only twelve dollars in central Illinois?

There are probably many things that caused that difference. These differences are more likely the root causes of the high cost of medical services. These are the things that are driving up the cost of medical insurance.

I do not hear people talking about or looking at these causes. They are only yelling that the costs are too high, therefore limiting the access to good medical help to those who have a lot of money.

One of the things that is driving up the cost of medical service is malpractice insurance. This is probably one of the reasons my doctor visit in Illinois was only twelve dollars and the same visit in California would have been at least fifty dollars.

I remember a visit I made to a doctor in California. This doctor had a part-time practice and the other part of his time he was a teacher at a medical school. He liked to have his practice so he could help people and also stay fresh in his skills of delivering health-care services.

When I was in his office, I noticed that he had an acupuncture chart on the wall. I asked him if he did acupuncture. He told me that he knew acupuncture but did not practice it. Wondering if there was some reason that he did not practice it, I asked him why he did not practice it. He told me it would cost him an extra twenty-five hundred dollars a month above what he was already paying for malpractice insurance if he were to practice it.

Now given that this doctor was only practicing medicine part-time, this could be a significant increase in what he would have to charge his patients. Let's assume that he only saw patients for fifty hours a month (as opposed to a full-time doctor doing about two hundred hours). He would have to charge an extra fifty dollars an hour to cover this cost.

Given that this was the cost to add another specialty to his practice, it would seem to me that his basic malpractice and other specialties that his malpractice insurance would already be much greater than that number. This would mean that to start with he would need to charge well in excess of fifty dollars an hour just for insurance. He would also have to charge for things like office space, equipment, staff, utilities, and so on. All this before he can make a profit. It is it any wonder that an office visit starts at fifty dollars or more?

Could this be one of the root causes of the high cost of medical services that people tend to overlook or choose to ignore?

Why are malpractice insurance rates so high? There are many factors that contribute to these costs.

While many, if not most, doctors are very competent and do a good job, there are some who are not that good or should not even be practicing medicine. There are medical associations and medical licensing boards that should be evaluating the abilities of doctors and removing those who are not qualified or who are dangerous to the public. These doctors end up in many malpractice lawsuits that cause insurance rates to go up for everyone.

Even the best doctors can occasionally have an unforeseen problem that may cause injury to a patient. This is where malpractice insurance is supposed to help protect the doctor from financial ruin. This is just like having auto insurance to help protect you from the financial loss due to an accident.

One of problems that has caused malpractice and other insurance rates to go up has been the excessive monetary judgments in court cases. While I am not saying that people should not be compensated for injuries, I do not think that many of the judgments that have come down lately are way beyond reasonable compensation for the injury. A good example is someone getting a million-dollar judgment for spilling a hot cup of coffee on themselves.

People are treating malpractice insurance as though it was were their own personal lottery where everyone else has to pay for their lottery ticket.

One way the lawyers have been able to get juries to award large settlements has been to talk about all the other people who will or may have been injured by the defendant. Thankfully, the Supreme Court has recently ruled that unless these other people are party to the litigation, they cannot be used in the discussion of damages. Since then I have heard that the rate at which insurance rates are going up has eased.

Another thing I seem to remember from my younger days is that lawyers did not do a lot of advertising on television. It seems to me that as these ads have increased and their claims of getting large settlements have grown, the insurance rates have also grown. While I am not saying this is a direct cause, it seems to me there might be a correlation.

Whatever the cause is, I do think these excessively large awards are a large contribution to the increase in malpractice insurance rates and ultimately the increasing cost of medical services. This again, is one of the root causes of the medical crisis everyone is trying to solve.

These large awards are also affecting those companies that make medicines and medical supplies. Many of these companies have to spend millions of dollars and many years to develop their products. In order to stay in business, they have to charge enough for their products to cover their development costs. Now they must add enough to their price to pay for insurance against these large settlements should someone find a defect that might occur. Depending on how widely the product might be used, this additional cost could be many times the cost of the product. This again increases the overall cost of health-care delivery.

With the legal system now making not only the companies that develop these medical supplies liable for their product but also their suppliers, these suppliers are also increasing their costs to medical companies to help them cover potential losses. I worked at a medical-supply company where companies that made raw materials the company used to make into medical products either refused to supply materials or greatly increased what they charged for the raw materials. They were forced to do this to be able to protect themselves from legal actions and unwarranted financial awards. This again increased the basic costs of the medical supplies.

I am sure many of the things I have been discussing also apply in the hospitals as well. All of this is pushing the cost of health-care delivery out of the reach of the average person, let alone those of lesser means.

Another thing I find interesting is that many of those who want the government to take over health care also say that we have some of the best health care in the world. In my opinion, one of the reasons for this is the profit motive for companies to try to develop new and better treatments for illnesses.

One of the reasons many people want the government to take over health-care insurance is that they want them to control costs. One of the politicians' favorite ways to try to control costs is to put a limit on what doctors and suppliers can charge for services. This means they will limit or possibly even eliminate the profit from products. Without the opportunity for profit, many companies will refrain from developing new procedures or equipment. Without this development, what has been considered one of the best health-care systems in the world would stagnate and fall behind. New development of medicines and equipment would be slowed and lives that might have been saved in the future would be lost. If we are interested in improving people's lives and saving lives, this would become very counterproductive.

On a recent TV show, Michael Moore was arguing with a person from the insurance industry. Mr. Moore was asking why the industry should make a profit from health insurance. I find it interesting that Mr. Moore was objecting to someone making a profit. I am sure that if his movies did not make a profit, he would not have nor could he get funding to produce his movies. Now we must consider that he is trying to put himself in the position of a doctor who is trying to cure the ills of the health-care system and making a profit and asking those in the health-care field not to make a profit. I find this position very two-faced and difficult to understand. If you do not agree with the profit motive, why should you profit from saying people should not make a profit?

What is socialized medicine? My *Random House College Dictionary* describes it as, "Any of various systems for providing the entire population with complete medical care through government subsidization of medical and health services."

One thing that happens when governments get involved is that politicians start arguing over what the government will do. This means that politicians instead of doctors will be making decisions on what medical treatments are appropriate. This also means that politicians will have more money to play with and use to their advantage. This will give them money to help reward their friends.

One of the arguments for the government to take over control of health care is to control the profit motive. This moves the profit motive from individuals, businesses to the politicians. They can profit from telling the people they know best how to run such a system to help get themselves elected. This can be seen in the number of presidential candidates who are using government health care as a major part of their campaigns. Once elected, they can profit from helping their friends get lucrative contracts. This means the politicians profit, but the suppliers of the services have limited profits to develop new procedures or medicines.

Also, with the government in charge, it means that a bureaucrat now becomes responsible for your medical care.

In a discussion, Mr. Moore (who is in favor of the government taking over health care) commented that the government agency FEMA was a good idea, but the man who was in charge during the New Orleans problem did not do a good job. What type of person does he think will run the health-care agency? Does he think that because the government takes over it will run any better than FEMA? Or how would he put it together so that there will not be the same problems? Will it be run any better than Social Security? Right now everyone is saying that Social Security will go bankrupt. The government does not seem to be able to correct that problem. A government-run health-care system would be large like

Social Security, Can the government and politicians guarantee that it will run any better or be any more solvent in the future?

As with Social Security, a government-run health-care system would mean that the individual would not have any choice in where he gets his services. The people would not have the choice to move to a different plan from a different group that may be better able to supply the service. No one would be able to look for a better provider.

Another interesting discussion I heard was that we need to stop calling the plan to have the government run health care "socialized medicine." I find that interesting given the dictionary definition I mentioned above. With this in mind, I wonder what their reasoning might be. Of course, in recent times there have been a lot of attempts to change the definition of many things. Is this not unlike calling daisies roses. We know that women like roses, but they are expensive. If we give them daisies and call them roses, it would be less expensive for the giver, and the receiver would be getting roses.

Do these people think by changing the name of the idea will make it more acceptable to the people and make the system work any better?

Let's take a look at this overall idea. We want to put our health-care system in the hands of the government. This is the same government that cannot run FEMA properly and rescue people in New Orleans in a timely manner. This is the same government that cannot keep Social Security solvent. This is the same government that cannot control the extreme financial awards in lawsuits that are driving up the cost of health care. This is the same government that cannot stop its politicians from spending billions on pork-barrel projects. This is the same government that is constitutionally charged with maintaining the "postal roads" and allows bridges to deteriorate and collapse.

What makes us think this government can do a better job at running the health-care system? And if the government cannot run it well, who can we turn to as an alternative? At least with our current system we can look for a different insurance company if the one we are with is not doing a good job.

The government could do more to help the healthcare system if it would work on things like bad doctors, ineffective medical procedures and exorbitant financial judgments against the system.

# Miscellaneous Ideas

Change is good? The dictionary defines change as "to be or cause to become different; alter." Other definitions include coinage or changing money for different denominations. I assume these others are not what the statement is talking about.

The definition says to become different; it does not talk about good or bad. The word "change" does not have any qualities. It does not have direction, color, flavor, or intensity. It only says that something is or will become different!

If we are to accept the phrase "change is good" every time we hear it, we have to accept that anything that is different is good. We have to accept that an airplane crashing is good because going from flying to crashing is a change, and change is good. The change from the government of Germany to the totalitarian government of Hitler was good because "change is good." The change from the idea of "innocent until proven guilty" to "because you might cause an accident or harm someone, you are guilty" is good because "change is good."

The idea that electronic means of enforcing the laws and the fact that you cannot question your accuser is better than having a person enforcing the law because "change is good."

One of the main reasons people seem to like the idea that change is good is that when someone talks about change, people tend to think it will be a change to their ideas. They do not look at the overall ramifications of the change, and they just focus on the part of the change they agree with.

Another miscellaneous idea is that of being alive or living. Part of the dictionary definition of "alive" is "having life; not extinct or inactive." The problem with these words is in how many people use and interpret them. It seems that many people think that just by having life and not being extinct or inactive is the most important thing.

A growing tree is alive and has its beauty. The major parts of its purpose are to create branches and a trunk to support its leaves. These leaves are then to perform photosynthesis, converting carbon dioxide to oxygen and taking nutrients and other things from the ground and converting them to other forms. When the tree stops doing these things, it is no longer living, even if its leaves are still green or there is still sap in its trunk.

A carrot pulled from the ground will maintain its green upper portion and its yellowish orange lower portion for a long time. Does this mean it is alive? It is no longer doing those natural functions it would normally do if it were truly living.

We humans take many different types of animals as pets. When these animals become unable to do the things they normally do because of serious illness or injury, we often make a decision that although the animal is alive, it is not truly living. If we cannot do anything to reverse these problems, we must make other decisions. In most cases, we will take pity and do the compassionate thing and put the animal to sleep. We understand that for it to just be alive is not be able to do most of the normal things it would do and does not constitute living or a quality life.

Each of us has his or her own set of ideas on what makes up our own quality of life. For some people, it is the ability to get away and go fishing. For others it is living in a big city and being able to go to a favorite restaurant or theater. For many of us it is having a home and family, but even in things like this, we each have our own ideas of what is perfect.

One thing most of us want is to be able to do these things and live the way we want without someone else telling us when, where, how, or if we are to do the thing we like.

Even our Founding Fathers understood this when in the Declaration of Independence they said:

> We hold these truths to be self-evident, that all men are created equal, that they are endowed by their Creator with certain unalienable Rights, that among these are Life, Liberty and the pursuit of Happiness.

They felt life was more than just being alive or existing. They felt we have the right to be able to live our own lives the way we see fit. In this statement, it is also implied that men do not have the right to interfere with other people's right to live their lives as they see fit.

This means that at the interface between people, one person's rights are not to be interfered with unless those rights would cause the other not to be able to exercise his rights. As an example, a person living in the city should not be able to tell the person in the country he should not go fishing because he is opposed to fishing. Nor should the person in the country be able to tell the person in the city he should not be able to go to the opera because he does not like opera.

In other words, no one should be able to put in place rules or laws regarding other people and how they live their life just based on their religious, moral, or other beliefs. Their ideas should not be laws unless there is some actual interference with another person's rights to life, liberty, or the pursuit of happiness.

This also means that one person's or group's rights do not include the right to tell others how they must live their lives. They do not have the right to say that because someone "might" do something that would interfere with another's rights they can control these activities.

If we continue to focus only on the perceived good or benefit of rules and laws and do not look at the interference with other people's rights, we will end up just existing. Will we have given away other's rights to life, liberty, and the pursuit of happiness? And in the process, will we not ultimately give up our own rights to life, liberty, and the pursuit of happiness because others will want to impose their own perceived good or benefits on us?

In the end, will we end up just existing, instead of living and enjoying our lives?

Another thought I have had is that freedom is like sitting down to a great steak (or your favorite) dinner. You sit there and enjoy the meal, and it gives you a very pleasurable feeling. Freedom also gives people a very pleasurable feeling. In fact, freedom is a very sought-after commodity for which people in many other countries have given up everything and even gambled their lives to move to a country where they feel they will have more freedom.

A great meal consists of an entree and other side dishes. All of these items are usually not served raw or in the form that they are first received in. The steak is broiled or barbecued. The potatoes and other vegetables are boiled or baked. These actions get the foods into a more eatable form that is more flavorful and easier to digest. Also, there are spices and other forms of flavor enhancement to help make the meal even more flavorful.

Freedom also needs some preparation. Here in America our Founding Fathers separated us from the rules of England. They then prepared our freedoms with the Constitution and the Bill of Rights. To enhance the experience, they allowed for amendments to the Constitution to allow for things (spices) they were not aware of at the time the Constitution was written. They also gave rights to the states to pass laws so they could adjust the "spices" to allow for regional differences and tastes.

Around my house, the Food Network is on quite frequently. There are many different chefs who prepare similar meals, but by using different spices in varying amounts, they change the flavor and style of the meal. They can take the same basic ingredients and make a meal with a Northeastern flavor or they can give it a Cajun flavor or even give it a Southwestern flavor. All of this can be done by varying the types and amounts of spices used. All of these different styles can produce a very delightful meal.

A similar thing can be said about the laws that are being passed to try to refine freedom and give it a "flavor" that best enhances the experience. But as with spices, laws need to be used sparingly. If we took a basic meal and then allowed every chef to come in and add the spices he would normally use, the amount and variation of spices would clash and overwhelm the flavor of the meal. In fact, the meal would be so overwhelmed by the spices, it would become inedible. The same is true with laws that are the spice of freedom. Excessive use of them tends to overwhelm the underlying freedom, and the more they are used, the less the "flavor" of freedom comes through.

One of the most common spices is salt. It is not only a common spice, but it is also something our body needs in small amounts. With freedom, this spice would be controlling other people. A little bit of control over what is acceptable in other people's behavior can help improve the "flavor" of freedom. An excessive amount of salt on a meal will not only make it less and less flavorful, but it can also make it dangerous to the person eating the meal because excessive salt can have a harmful effect on the body. It is the same with laws controlling other people. When these laws start controlling other people's actions to the extent that it starts to limit their individual freedoms, it also starts becoming damaging to the "body's" freedom.

Maybe this is why many great thinkers and our Founding Fathers felt large governments with lots of laws were not the way to go.

To paraphrase people like Henry David Thoreau and Thomas Paine, "He who governs best, governs least." Another good quote is, "Too many cooks spoil the broth."

We are becoming a health-conscious country but what about the health of the country. We are seeing many initiatives that want more disclosure as to what is in our food. These initiatives are trying to get more reporting on the amounts of fats, sodium, trans-fats, dyes, sugar, and other specific items in our foods.

This initiative has been going on for some time, and we are seeing greater disclosure of the things in our food.

Now that we are seeing what is in our food, a new set of initiatives is now being pushed. These initiatives are saying how much of things such as trans-fats and salt are to be allowed in food. Also, there are initiatives that are saying what food items are allowed in our schools based on certain limits on the amounts of various items in them. This is all being done with the intent of improving the health of our youth.

Now as I am watching the stories on this, I am wondering, if we need to control the content of the foods our children are getting in school, shouldn't we apply these same rules to the health of our freedoms?

Would it not make the same sense for us to set standards on the laws that our politicians are producing? They are creating laws to control people's actions that are not much different than companies adding sodium to foods to get a desired result. Should we not have initiatives to set limits on how much control the government should have the same as the limits we are putting on the additives that are allowed in our food?

Seeing that our government is now attacking food as any other narcotic, what is next on their list? I am sure it is not the narcotic of politics.

Our Founding Fathers were able to establish the foundation for our country in a few pages. In these pages they were able to put together a framework of the basic laws that were to govern the whole country. If they were able to do this together in a few pages, maybe we should limit the rest of the laws to a thousand pages instead of the volumes that fill large rooms we now have. Maybe we should reduce our politicians' salaries by an amount proportional to the number of words in laws they pass and increase their salary by the number of words they remove from the law books.

This idea has some merit, as some state legislatures have a time limit on how long their legislative sessions are to last. After this time limit, the amounts of things like their per diem are reduced. This does two things. It encourages them to get their work done in a timely manner, and it also pushes them to work on the more important items and not waste a lot of time on marginal laws.

There is a large group of people who are trying to get everyone to go back to more natural foods in order to enhance our physical well being. We should also be pushing to go back to the basic ideas our Founding Fathers put forth to help improve the health of our freedoms and the emotional health of our people. The more rules and laws our politicians pass, the more stress they are going to generate among the people and the less freedoms we will have.

Another thing that needs to be considered is the people and bureaucrats that are involved in designing the roads and establishing traffic control.

As I have talk about elsewhere, I feel education is one of the best methods of helping reduce traffic accidents and other problems. That this also applies to those doing the designs and setting the rules.

I talk about the fact that if people would learn to keep to the right on the freeways, there would probably be less road rage and therefore fewer accidents. On a recent trip, I realized the designers of freeways are doing things that make this more difficult. One thing they have done is to suddenly take what had been a traffic lane for many miles and past many exits, and make it an exit off of the freeway. If we want people (especially slower traffic) to keep to the right, why do we take this lane and suddenly turn it into an exit? At this point, there is probably a considerable amount of traffic that is not keeping to the right, and therefore when you suddenly find you are on an exit, you have no way of moving to the through lane.

I feel this type of design also contributed to the bus accident that occurred in Atlanta, Georgia, that killed and injured a number of college baseball players. The bus driver was traveling down the freeway in the carpool lane and was keeping to the left on the freeway. He probably did not realize that that lane would suddenly become an exit. He probably assumed, as I would, that a lane that had been going on for a long distance was a through lane and did not expect it to suddenly become an exit.

The designers of freeway exits should always create a new lane that is clearly indicated as being an exit only lane. If the number of lanes is to be reduced, the left lanes should be the ones to be well marked and removed. This would help encourage people to keep to the right, and also if people were keeping to the right, this would affect a smaller number of drivers.

Speaking of carpool or HOV lanes, I do a lot of traveling in different cities and even though there are usually two of us in the car, I usually do not get into these lanes for many reasons. One reason is that I usually am not familiar enough with the roads in these areas, and I am worried about trying to get out of the lane when I need to get to an exit I need. Also, I am worried about trying to get across many lanes of traffic to get to that exit. Another problem is that these lanes are usually only one lane wide and if you get behind someone who may be nervous about the traffic and cannot keep up to the appropriate speed, there is no way to get around them. Also, being only one lane, if there is an accident, it is more likely to block the lane and make it impossible to get around them. It also bothers me that I should be staying to the right and allowing other traffic to have the opportunity to properly pass me on the left.

I also feel that for the cost of these lanes and the special exits, the money could have been better spent to put two extra lanes on the main road to give everyone a better drive. I do not think the amount of extra carpooling has reduced the amount of traffic proportional to the cost. I also feel these HOV lanes have added to the stress and confusion of how to properly drive on the freeways.

Another miscellaneous idea I would like to discuss is "zero tolerance." We have many schools in this country that are instituting a zero-tolerance policy.

They are saying that certain things are not allowed on the school campus. They define things the students cannot have on campus, but students see teachers and others on campus with these items. Is this not teaching them there is a double standard, and others should do as I say and not as I do? This is also teaching them that the rules do not apply equally to everyone. Of course this means we are teaching them that the fundamental ideas of the Declaration of Independence and the Constitution do not apply to everyone. It is teaching them that we do not all have equal rights under the Constitution.

Many schools have an absolute policy that guns and drugs are not allowed on campus, yet they will invite people in to show drugs to the children. They will also have or allow security guards with guns or police carrying guns on their campus. This also teaches them that laws or rules need not always be followed. This is teaching them that rules are made to be broken.

And as to the fact that police and others are allowed to carry a gun onto school grounds, does this not imply that anyone who is allowed to carry a gun also has the right to carry a gun onto school property? The police, when they are not in "hot pursuit," are no different than any other citizen.

Among the side effects of a society where everyone is trying to control everything is the current push to have everyone use germicidal soaps and wipes. While on the surface this might sound like a great idea, this could have a downside.

Many of you may remember the story of the boy in the bubble. This was the story of a boy who had a defect that prohibited his immune system from developing. His immune system did not develop the capability of fighting off germs. Humans' immune systems are very limited when they are born. The immune system develops all through life to detect low levels of germs and create immunities to these germs.

While sanitation is an important part of keeping healthy, excessive use of germicides could lead to a greater problem. As I have said, the immune system learns from the germs that it comes in contact with. If a child is brought up in a home or other environment that has been so sanitized that his immune system is not able to develop immunities to the many normal germs, he would become more susceptible to infection. Leaving the sanitary environment he was brought up in would be like the boy in the bubble leaving his protective room. Any contact with the germs he had been protected from as a child could produce illnesses far greater than those experienced by people brought up in less germicidal environments. The sudden onslaught of normal germs that he had not developed any immunity to could overwhelm his body.

This is not unlike the problem that sheep shearers have with the excessive softening of their hands due to the lanolin in the sheep's wool. Those shearers who do not wear gloves soon find their hands become so softened by the lanolin that trying to pick up or touch anything could be a very painful experience.

# *Conclusion*

What happens if we ignore what our Founding Fathers envisioned and put into motion? We can look around at many other countries that were not founded on the principles ours was started on. The main principle comes from the Declaration of Independence. "We hold these truths to be self-evident, that all men are created equal, that they are endowed by their Creator with certain unalienable Rights, that among these are Life, Liberty and the pursuit of Happiness." This principle indicates that the most important part of the country is the people and their happiness.

As people and governments start to ignore this principle, the fabric of the government and the welfare of the people starts to unravel. This has been demonstrated over and over in history as we have seen and watched governments and political structures collapse in on themselves. These governments tend to disappear and unfortunately, they are replaced with new governments that have not learned from the mistakes of their predecessors.

Let's look at some of the indicators that begin to appear when a government is starting to collapse. There are many indicators that are obvious when we look back. There are things such as political infighting, corruption, and ignoring the needs of the people. There are more subtle indicators that are not so obvious but are nonetheless indicative of the coming collapse of the political structure.

All of these can be found in the subtle changes in the daily activities of the people. These are changes where the people are not being fulfilled with their lives and start to look for other things to help them feel fulfilled or otherwise to enjoy their lives.

The problem stems from the fact that the government or those in charge start sucking the life out of the people. All people have a notion about how they want to live their lives. As the government pushes their ideas of how people should live their lives, the people find less and less enjoyment in their daily lives.

To offset this loss of enjoyment, people will start spending more time on those fewer things in which they can find enjoyment.

One thing we are now becoming aware of is obesity in our country. Is this an indicator? Well, many, if not most, people find food enjoyable to some extent. As there are less and less enjoyments in their lives, they tend to spend more time eating.

Alcohol is another thing many people find enjoyable. Is this an indicator? Let's look at the Soviet Union. One major problem that grew as the government took more control and became more corrupt was the fact that many of their people were becoming alcoholics.

Food and alcohol have been around for years and their usage can be tracked through time. There have always been people who have abused these things. If you tracked how widespread their abuse became as compared to the decline of their governments, you would find a strong correlation. I am not saying that increased abuse caused the decline of the government. What I am saying is that the more the governments interfered with people's right to enjoy their lives, the more the abuse.

I have not mentioned other drugs. Many of these have only become readily available in more recent times. Therefore the amount of history we have with these is not as extensive, but we can see the same correlation.

In this country, we have many people who are trying to fight, control, or eliminate the abuses of many substances. There are people struggling to figure out how to fight obesity in our country. They want to eliminate tobacco. They are fighting the drug problems. They are fighting alcohol abuse. They are fighting crime. They are doing all of these things by trying to get more laws passed. They want the government to take more control of people's lives.

My question is are we attacking the problem or are we causing more of a problem? As I have said, our Founding Fathers thought people had the right to life, liberty, and the pursuit of happiness. They did not say the government had the right to interfere with people's right to have an enjoyable life.

The Founding Fathers had a deep understanding of people. If they were still around, they would stop attacking the indicators of a country in decline and start attacking those things that are causing the decline. They would be less interested in trying to interfere with people's individual lives and more interested in attacking those things interfering with people's lives. They would be trying to get the government out of the people's lives and allowing them to enjoy their lives instead of looking for enjoyment elsewhere.

Our Founding Fathers struggled with the idea that the people were the most important. They felt so strongly about this idea that they declared their independence from a government that did not share that view. If they were under control of a government like we have now, I believe they would again declare their independence.

At the time of the writing of this section, I had already written the great majority of this book. Several times during this writing I had thought about Ben Franklin. I seemed to remember that he had published something called *Common Sense*. I decided to try to locate some information on this, but I was surprised to find that he did publish it, but Thomas Paine originally wrote it.

This document was written back when the idea of separation from England was just starting to take hold. I decided to sit down and read this document to see what was going on back then. I did know that many of the reasons for the separation from England were based on taxes and the king imposing his will on the people without regard to people's rights or needs for freedom from excessive control.

While the style of writing back in the 1700s made it a little difficult to read, I was surprised at what I found. I found that it was not a tirade against the king of England, but instead I found it to be a discussion of the history of monarchies along with the good and bad of that form of government. In fact, in general it is a discussion of all forms of government and the problems they create.

He did this very eloquently while trying not to make any judgments on what was right or wrong. He was trying to make the reader think about what he was saying without alienating anyone with his judgments. This was surprising to me because that was in part what I have been trying to do in this writing. I have never professed to be a writer or public speaker, so I am sure my writings are far from being as eloquent as his are.

I was also surprised to find that many things he chose to discuss and in many cases the way he discussed them were very similar to what I have said.

In his discussions of government, I have found many of the same concerns I have tried to raise here. While much of his discussion is based on monarchies, a lot of what he has to say can be applied to any form of government. In fact, it can be seen from his discussions that this document had a very great influence on the Declaration of Independence and ultimately on the basis of the Constitution.

While he did spend a lot of time on the discussion of the fact that the colonies had all the necessary elements to be able to form a sustainable country, the rest of the document covered other ideas. He not only discussed what was wrong with the existing government, but he also gave ideas on how a better government could be formed. In later publications, he tried to show some groups who were opposed to the idea of separation that their arguments in themselves were also valid for that separation. He showed that while arguing for reconciliation, they were using arguments that showed the need for separation.

The *Common Sense* document was exceedingly well accepted and widely read in Paine's time. Remember, there were not as many people back then and many of them did not know how to read. Considering this, the publication of one hundred thousand copies could be considered astronomical for that time.

Another comment I would like to make on Thomas Paine and his writing of *Common Sense* is that I think this document exemplifies the difference between a politician and what I would call a statesman. Yes, he had an objective in mind. He felt strongly that the colonies should break their ties to England. But he did not go out and start shouting that everyone should listen to him and just believe he had the right answer. He did not try to say he was doing it for the kids and that everyone needed to agree with him because of that. He did not go out and solicit endorsements from this group or that group to be able to say that he had a number of people supporting his idea. He instead created a discussion about why it needed to be done. He gave examples of the pros and cons of the idea. He discussed the historical implications of where they were at that time. He presented the case that all the necessary elements were there to form the new government. And as to the form of government that needed to be created, he made a suggestion as to what form it should take. He made suggestions as to what should be included and what should not be included. He understood he was not the only one who had good ideas. In fact, he was trying to draw out ideas. He wanted everyone to have the advantage of the best-possible ideas.

This is a far cry from the current political arena. This is a far cry from politicians who feel their answers are the best without really considering the impact on the individual's rights. After all, the government of our Founding Fathers and suggested in the work *Common Sense* was one in which individual rights were to be supreme as long as those rights did not diminish the rights of others.

What both Paine and the other statesmen did not do is to define the government as one that was responsible for the success or failure of the people. They did not define what should be considered success or failure. They tried to define a government whose responsibility it was to provide the things necessary for people to find their own success and failure. They knew people needed to be secure, so they said the government needed to provide an army and navy to protect Americans from external forces. They knew they needed to provide infrastructure to facilitate commerce among the people. They thought the government should only provide the things necessary to give the people the ability make their own way. They did not try to define right or wrong. They only said that the individual's rights must be protected. This, by implication, meant that when anyone's rights were diminished by giving someone else more rights, it was wrong. This also implied the government should not be in the business of defining arbitrary rights. They also said government officials should not be held any higher than the other citizens. These people were given the job of protecting the people's rights, not defining their rights. They were not to have any more rights than those required to do their job. In times of peace, the militia did not have the right to occupy anyone's property without consent and/or payment for its use. This meant they were no different than any other citizen.

I think if these statesmen were around today, they would view our current government and political landscape as not being that different than how Mr. Paine viewed the government he wanted to separate from.

I have been writing this document under a working title. After reading the work of Mr. Paine, I am considering changing the title to reflect his document. I do not consider this to be plagiarizing his title but rather a mark of respect to his eloquent writings that were trying to get the people of his time to look at their government as I am trying to do today.

978-0-595-46578-1
0-595-46578-1